The BELOVED

Rano Gayley 1972

The BELOVED

The Life and Work of Meher Baba

by

Naosherwan Anzar

Sheriar Press, Inc.

NORTH MYRTLE BEACH, S.C.

Publisher

Sheriar Press, Inc.
North Myrtle Beach, S.C., 29582

Printed in the United States

DEDICATION

Why did I write this book? I could give the answer in three words: I had to. How else do you express gratitude to a man who fills the whole span of your life, a man who has more than your faith, who has transmitted to you a conviction. A conviction of his Avatarhood. I have known Meher Baba for over twenty years; I was a child when it all began. Then I looked up at him as a happy, joyous and cheerful man. As I grew up, I was drawn to him not irrationally, but with candour. That was his greatest trait: he gave those who believed in him a sense of fellowship. To walk hand in hand, through turmoil and terror and through temptation and to find peace — this is what the Avatar has described as God's gift to the faithful. Baba had bestowed on me a glimpse of that blessedness. I had met him many a time — in my family home where he would come, in Meherazad where I'd go and see him, talk to him, sit with him. I want to share that experience. Hence this book.

The faithful have a bias for the God-Man. Understandably so, because the bias is made of love. I do not believe that can hurt the objectivity of a biography. His life was an open book. It was a forceful book. Many who had at one time or other questioned his words, his acts, came to bow down at his feet and weep in joy, in love, in peace. It is fortunate that he came in an age where the camera had been invented, where photographs could be recorded. The photographs speak for the God-Man; photographs have no bias.

The photographs also show the human form. They show him walking, talking, leaning on crutches — a man who would suffer, a man who would not speak for forty years. Being alive is biological. But living for others, living to give love and peace is divinity, and it is also a crucifixion. Masters suffer for humanity, but the Avatar suffers for one and all beings and things, and is crucified, so that man can find his place among other men and in the Universe in terms of love.

Today the journey goes on; the size of the procession swells every year. They come from all over the world to trek to that little abode on the top of a stony hill. Because he is there. They call it *Darshan*. There is no past tense when you talk of Meher Baba, there is no history. He is here, now. The photographs, the memories are only a preface to an Experience.

There is still some more. In this age of technology, science breeds her own curse. There is degeneration and decay of the mind through addictions and drugs. Yet there is hope because there are crusaders who speak of hope. Many of them have dipped into the spring of Baba's love. Others will follow. Maybe some will because this book inspired them. To all those waiting to join hands, I dedicate this work of love.

ACKNOWLEDGEMENTS

'The Beloved' is essentially a pictorial biography of Meher Baba. Despite the fairly detailed text with marginal comments, it makes no claim of being exhaustive.

Collecting and collating the material, which has been scattered all around, has been a very difficult though interesting process. It has taken me a number of years to do it. While I have tried to illustrate Meher Baba's life, as far as possible, in his own words, my information is based largely on the diaries of the disciples who lived and travelled with him.

I am grateful to hundreds of individuals whose experiences and narrations have helped me in making this book possible. My basic material has been the diaries and notes (both published and unpublished) of C. B. Purdom, F. H. Dadachanji, Dr. A. G. Munsiff, Ramjoo Abdulla, K. J. Dastur, Jal S. Irani, Mani S. Irani, Kitty L. Davy, Filis Frederick and Norina Matchabelli. To all of them I am most indebted.

Very grateful thanks to Sufism Reoriented, Inc. for permitting me to quote from *God Speaks*, *Listen, Humanity*, and *Life At Its Best* by Meher Baba and to Meher Spiritual Center, Inc. for permission to use information contained in *The God-Man* by C. B. Purdom.

A special word of gratitude to Pradip Paul, Adi K. Irani and Eruch Jessawala whose constant help, guidance and cooperation have been invaluable.

I owe much to my mother and father without whose encouragement this work would not have emerged in print.

Naosherwan Anzar

BOMBAY
INDIA
July 10, 1972

TABLE of CONTENTS

FAMILY TREE

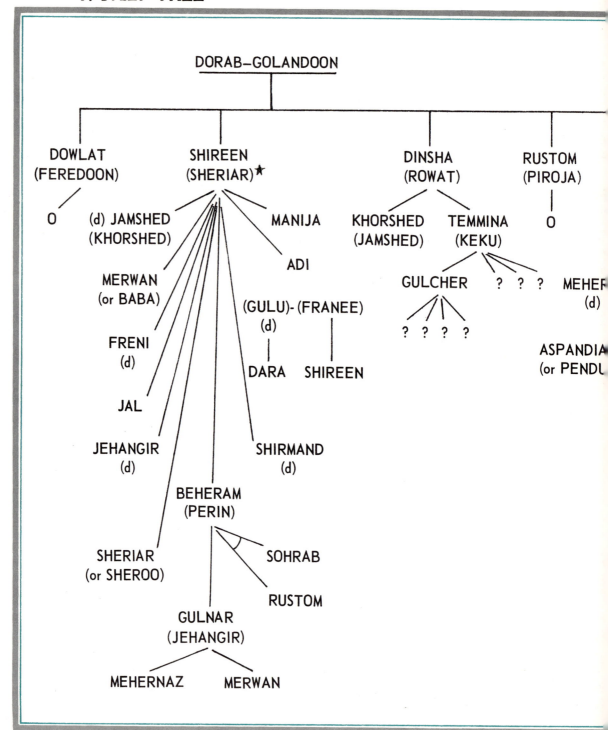

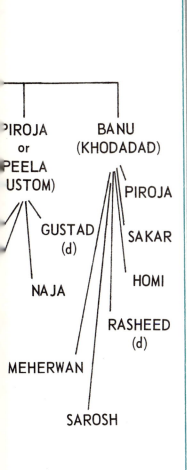

PIROJA
or
PEELA
USTOM)

GUSTAD
(d)

NAJA

MEHERWAN

SAROSH

BANU
(KHODADAD)

PIROJA

SAKAR

HOMI

RASHEED
(d)

d: died

APPROXIMATE DATES OF IMPORTANT EVENTS

1853	Sheriar was born in Iran in Khooramshar.
1858	Sheriar's mother died in Iran.
1865	At the age of 12 Sheriar left home.
1873	For eight years Sheriar led an ascetic life in Iran.
1873 - 74	When barely 21 years of age Sheriar left Iran for India.
1878	Shireen was born in India.
1873 - 83	For nearly 10 years Sheriar continued his life of a dervish (ascetic) in India.
1883	Sheriar became engaged to Shireen, a girl of 5 .
1883 - 92	Sheriar remained engaged to Shireen for 9 years.
1892	★ Sheriar married Shireen at 14 years of age.
1893	First child son, Jamshed was born.
1894	Second child son, MERWAN was born on February 25.
1902	Son, Jal born on September 15.
1908	Son, Beheram born on June 20.
1914	Son, Adi born on July 10.
1918	Last child daughter, Manija born on December 15. (Sheriar was then 65 and Shireen was 40 years of age.)
1932	Sheriar died (in Bombay) at the age of 79 on April 30.
1943	Shireen died (in Poona) at the age of 65 on February 25.

"I and the Truth which I bring are inseparable, one from the other. I am one with the Truth. May you all, too, break through the numberless cages and realize that you are one with the limitless Truth of divine life. The divine Beloved is always with you, in you and around you."

Meher Baba
1894 - 1969

THE BELOVED

The ascent to the hill at Meherabad is not too cumbersome. Large mounds of small hillocks seem to spread out in waves, and underfoot the trail is a slew of sharp-edged rocks. For miles around there is ethereal silence, broken by the rustling of a solitary tree edging itself over a craggy rock. I could see from lower Meherabad the white dome of the Tomb. It seemed to emerge like the sun from the line of horizon. [1]

I had come immediately after I got the news. As I plodded up the hill, I remembered. He had looked at me with compassion. I had clutched his feet and embraced his body. Without any apparent reason my eyes had welled up tears, and before I could step out of the room Meher Baba had pointed to his wrist and said, "My time has come" and then making a cross with his fingers he had remarked, "This is my crucifixion." That was my last meeting with him in that little corner room at Meherazad in Ahmednagar District, India, in the evening of December 23, 1968.

Forty days later I received the telegram from Baba's secretary Adi K. Irani: "AVATAR MEHER BABA DROPPED HIS PHYSICAL BODY AT TWELVE NOON 31ST JANUARY AT MEHERAZAD TO LIVE ETERNALLY IN THE HEARTS OF HIS LOVERS." That very day in the evening his disciples — the mandali — had carried his body from Meherazad to be placed in the crypt of the Tomb at Meherabad. Meher Baba had hinted to them on that last day, the morning of January 31, that seven days later, "he would be 100 per cent free." Exactly seven days later, at 12:15 noon on Friday, February 7, 1969, the Beloved was interred amidst the resonant cries of 'Avatar Meher Baba Ki Jai' (Hail Avatar Meher Baba).

Meher Baba's Tomb on Meherabad Hill

[1] The Tomb was built by Meher Baba's direction in 1927 over a site where he had sat in seclusion in the early days at Meherabad. (It was then called the Dome because of its unique architecture.) The interior was painted with murals by the Swiss artist Helen Dahm in 1937.

When he was born, they called him Merwan. His other name, Meher Baba, would come many years later. The date was recorded by the Zoroastrian Calendar: Tir Roj, the month of Meher, 1263 Yezdezardi. His parents were Zoroastrians and they were faithful to the customs. February 25th, 1894, Sunday, 5:00 a.m. The moment of the Avatar.

Was there a clue to his birth? A seed, a premonition? Yes, the seed was born forty-one years before. We shall have to go back to 1853 and Khoramsha, a small town in Iran. That was the birth of his father, Sheriar Mundegar Irani.

Right from his birth, Sheriar's life seemed to have been ordained. The family he was born into had a mystic air. His father Mundegar was the keeper of the Tower of Silence (the place where Zoroastrians place their dead). His mother died when he was only five. There was nobody to look after the child at home. His father would take him to the Tower; the boy watched the prayers and the rituals. The foundation was being laid. [2]

At the age of thirteen, strangely drawn to the life of a mystic, Sheriar left home in search of God. For eight long years he roamed Iran as an itinerant monk. He travelled from place to place on foot, slept wherever he could get shelter and asked for food when hunger compelled him to do so.

Years rolled on. He had not found what he was looking for. Disillusioned, he looked for an escape. His brother Khodadad was about to leave for India. Sheriar decided to join the party. We don't know much about the journey, except that it was long and hazardous. In Bombay Khodadad took up a job. [3] Sheriar too looked for jobs, but would not keep them long. The unfulfilled search burned inside him and he started travelling around on foot. He went to Karachi, stayed there a month and continued his journey through the barren wastelands of Gujarat and Kutch.

One day while walking through a desert, foot-weary and worn out, Sheriar was overcome by unbearable thirst. He could walk no further and swooned. When he woke up, he saw two men, an aged fakir and a younger man, standing beside him. They offered him water from their leather bag. One of them said: "Why have you come here? Why should you trouble God by acting foolishly? Now go on your way and you will come across a hut where an old man will give you food to eat. Then proceed in the opposite direction and you will reach a town."

[2] One day Sheriar was sitting on the grounds of the 'Tower of Silence,' when he saw a figure running up the cobbled path. As the figure came closer he saw that it was a young and beautiful Irani woman running in fright. In a state of exhaustion she explained that some Mohammedans were chasing her and begged him to save her. Nearby where he was sitting was an oven (a large urn-like opening in which the relatives of the dead baked their bread), and since it had not been used that day it was cold. He helped the trembling girl into the urn and placed the lid on it. Before long he heard the hoofs of galloping horses and a group of Mohammedan riders came in view and asked him if he had seen any one pass by a few minutes ago. Sheriar replied that he had been there for over an hour, and not a dog had passed by. They felt he was speaking the truth (which indeed he was!) and turning about they galloped off. Sheriar let the woman out of the oven and escorted her home.

[3] Khodadad lived half the time in India and half the time in Iran. He was a short-statured man with a short white beard, small beady eyes and he was very parsimonious. He loved Baba intensely and never failed to see him when he could on his visits to India. Strangely enough he never used a vehicle where his legs could carry him. On his visits to Meherabad, Baba would send the little tonga (horse carriage) to the station to fetch him. But he would insist on trudging the distance, alongside the empty tonga. At the most he would be persuaded to place his bundle in the tonga to enable him to walk unburdened.

Sheriar raised his head to thank his benefactors, but to his astonishment he found that the two men were not there and for miles around him there was no sign of life. "They are men from God" he thought. At last, here was a trail. He knelt down on the ground and prayed in gratitude.

The trail went on; there would be other clues, other visitations. Once, walking through the hills, Sheriar met an old man sitting in meditation. He approached the saintly man and saluted him. The old man looked up and said: "What do you want?" "Nothing," Sheriar answered. It was a strange answer, but the old man was pleased.

Sheriar continued his wanderings. He had not yet found his goal, he had not found God. He tried the hard way now — forty days of continuous meditation without food or sleep. But he couldn't complete the forty days. Before thirty days were over, strange things had happened. One night from sheer exhaustion he had dropped off to sleep by the side of a river when a voice spoke to him loud and clear: "You are not destined for that which you seek, but the one who will be born to you will achieve it. Rise and return home." Sheriar's racing heart told him it was the voice of God. He would have to do as the voice had commanded. Sheriar started for home. Home was now where his sister Piroja lived — in Poona.⁴

Piroja was overjoyed. Her long-lost brother had come back. She had adored him and when he left home, it had hurt her. Now the lost sheep had come back. She would have to help him stay back, help him to strike roots. She asked her brother to marry. Sheriar wouldn't agree, marriage was too strong a hold, it made him afraid. Then one day a peculiar thing happened. He was standing near the door of his house; he saw a little girl of five, clutching her slate, pass by. She was dressed in a short frock and her favourite red 'yar' (loose quarter length trousers) with a red ribbon at the end of her pigtail. Sheriar pointed at the little girl and said to his sister, "Alright, if I marry, I marry her and none else."

He chuckled at the absurdity of his proposition. May be he had meant it as a joke, to put an end to his sister's further coaxing. He was stunned when his sister took him up on it. Piroja knew her brother would never go back on his word and promptly went to see Golendoon, the mother of that child whose name was Shireen. She narrated the incident of that morning and begged her "on her knees" to save her brother and her happiness by consenting to

Sheriar Mundegar Irani, Meher Baba's father, was a Zoroastrian by birth and a mystic by choice.

⁴ Rustom (Baba's mother's brother) was a tall and handsome man, whose vocation and love was the theatre. He loved Baba very dearly and at the time of dying told his wife, Piroja, "I have always felt Baba is God — now I am convinced." Piroja, on one of her visits to Meherazad, requested the mandali with endearing simplicity to ask Baba to give her "Murti." The mandali who knew that she meant "Mukti" (salvation), asked her if she knew what it meant. She replied, "No, but I know it is something that Baba gives to his close ones, and after all I am his aunt. I know I am not good enough to deserve it, I do take snuff and sometimes swear, but I am sure he will overlook that, for I am his aunt."

3

5 Dorabjee (Shireen's father) had a good knowledge of herbs and dispensed free medicines and advice to the ailing. One day a patient came complaining of long-standing aches and pains, cold and fever. Dorabjee was sitting discussing a different matter with his friends, and since the patient had come once too often, he in a sense of fun prescribed exactly the opposite of what could help the man: take a cold bath, eat a seer of sour curds and sleep in the open covered with a wet sheet. The patient took the advice very seriously. A few days later he came back with deep gratitude for having been cured completely! Dorabjee was dumbfounded, but resolved never to joke again. (No doubt it was the man's faith that cured him.)

Shireen Sheriar Irani, Meher Baba's mother, was devoted to her family and loved Merwan intensely.

give her five-year-old daughter Shireen in marriage to the thirty-year-old Sheriar. Golendoon's husband raged and raved when he came home and heard what his wife had done, but word had been given, it was sacrosanct. 5

The next nine years was a period of readjustments, to living in society, to setting up house and to waiting for his little bride to grow up. Shireen grew up. When she was fourteen, they were married. At fifteen, her first child was born. The boy was named Jamshed.

Sheriar was a devoted husband and a kind father. Although in his earlier days he had renounced all material goods, he now decided to set up a toddy shop to maintain his family. The business was fairly successful and Sheriar even bought a small house out of his savings. The neighbours used to call it the "Pumpkin House" because at one side of the entrance there was a big round stone. Later they would buy a larger house (this was marked as "the house with the well").

Sheriar had implicit faith in the goodness of his friends and fellow-beings. This would cause him a lot of heartburn in his old age. He was getting infirm; the shop duties were heavy. He took in a young man called M as his partner. The partner would look after the business in the shop, while Sheriar attended to the auction of toddy tree lots which were purchased for the season. Gradually he handed over this part of the business as well to M and later, all that was required of him was his signature.

One evening M invited Sheriar to his house for dinner and served him with his favourite delectable Persian dishes. It was an evening of gay camaraderie and as Sheriar was about to leave, M placed "an official looking" typed sheet of paper before him and asked him to sign it saying that it was another toddy lot deal to be procured. Sheriar signed on the dotted line.

What he did not know was that the document he had put his name on declared that he had "unconditionally handed over as gift to M his share and part of the business." M soon staked his claim. The issue went before the courts. The total burden of looking after the legal matters fell on Shireen. She had to fight a lone battle — against the sharks and her husband's gullibility. Sheriar would say, "We are not the losers, what have we to lose? It is poor M himself. He has gained nothing and naturally has to suffer in many lives to come, just think of that! Can you see now why I am sorry for him? The law of cause and effect, of sow and reap is as inexorable as that — the laws of God are finer than the hair of our head." Shireen wouldn't understand this. "But who is going to see that?", she would say. "I will be dead, and if I see him in the next life I would not know it is M! Besides, what good is his suffering going to do to me? We have lost all the business, and whatever is in the bank (in cash and jewellery) for our children and their future will all be lost in court expenses!"

At seventy Sheriar would go to court with the name of 'Yazdan' on his lips, till one day the court finally ruled in M's favour. The judge stated that Sheriar was innocent and that he had been duped, but the fact remained that he had signed the document.

When it was all over, Sheriar sent a message to M saying, "I forgive you fully, some day you may want to ask my forgiveness and would not be able to do so, for I am an old man and would be dead by then. So remember you will not need my forgiveness, for I have forgiven you completely. It is now simply a matter between you and God."[6]

[6] In 1960 when Meher Baba was at Guruprasad in Poona, M's wife came on one of the darshan days and falling at his feet she cried and asked for forgiveness. She said that her husband had been bed-ridden for some time before his death and had repeatedly asked for Baba's forgiveness. Her husband was dead, and now she had come to do what his soul had yearned for. Baba lovingly caressed her tear-stained face, embraced her and told her not to worry and asked her to forget the episode. All was forgiven.

Meher Baba was born at Sassoon Hospital, Poona, on February 25, 1894. The slab commemorates his place of birth.

Merwan's Boyhood

There were no miracles, no signs that heralded Merwan's nativity, although, before his birth, Shireen had an unusual dream. She had dreamt being led into a wide open area where she was surrounded by a large number of alien faces, a multitude that extended on all sides to the horizon. The faces stared at her steadily and expectantly till she woke up and narrated the dream to those around her. The dream was interpreted as symbolising the birth of one who would be loved and esteemed by large multitudes.

7
Shireen called Merwan her "most beautiful child." He had the most lovely golden hair which she did not have the heart to cut and Merwan sported curls up to his shoulders till he was nearly five. He was often taken by strangers for a handsome European child. Shireen had an ambition that when Merwan would be older she would send him to England and Europe for further studies.

"Merwan was very active and mischievous from the time he was able to toddle, and would walk out of the house when my attention was distracted. This often compelled me, when I was especially busy with housework, or had to go for my bath and there was no one in the house to look after him, to tie one end of my sari to his waist and the other to the bedstead. Even then I could not always keep him out of mischief. Once I had left him playing on the floor. Returning to the room some minutes later I was horrified to see him playing merrily with a big black snake. With a piercing scream I rushed forward, but the snake slipped quickly out of the house and was never seen again."
                                                      Shireen

Merwan was very alert, a fast walker and an equally fast sprinter. Because of his sporting qualities, his friends called him 'Electricity.' When Merwan was twelve years of age, his father mentioned to him of having witnessed an unusual phenomenon at night at the Tower of Silence. Merwan too decided to go there. His friend, Behli J. Irani accompanied him one night at 11:30, without even a lantern. Behli was scared and wanted to retrace his steps, but Merwan boldly insisted on going to the very place where the corpses were placed. No sooner did they ascend the flight of stairs when they saw a tall man, in a white robe and a long white beard standing against the main door with hands outstretched. As the two of them approached the figure, it disappeared and the boys returned home after this strange and exciting adventure.

Merwan spent his childhood at 816, Butler Moholla, in Poona, and had a happy childhood.[7] At the age of five, he was admitted to the Dastur Girls' School and later studied for another five years at Camp Government English School.[8] He matriculated in 1911 from the St. Vincents' High School. He was seventeen then.

He had a deep interest in literature, especially poetry. He liked Shakespeare, Shelley and Wordsworth and was particularly attracted to the poetry of Shams al-Din, known as Hafiz. He wrote too, mainly poems in Gujarati, Urdu, Hindustani and Persian which were were published in Sanj Vartman, one of the popular Gujarati papers of Bombay. He wrote under the pen name of 'Homa.' He sang 'monajats,' Persian songs, and verses from the 'Avesta' in a soft, mellifluous voice.

Merwan in 1899

Meher Baba's house in Poona was called 'Pumpkin House' because on one side of the entrance there was a big round stone.

Merwan in 1917. L to r: Merwan, Behram, Khodadad, Jal, Adi Jr., Shireen, Jamshed

Merwan in 1913 when he met Hazrat Babajan who gave him the key to self-realization

Hazrat Babajan was a Perfect Master and even till this day people accept her as a saint and a God-realised being.

It was a morning of May. The year was 1913. Merwan had been going to college for two years. On this day he was on his way to college on a bicycle down Rao Saheb Kedari Road. Then he saw an old woman sitting under a neem tree. She beckoned to him. He stopped and got off his bicycle. When he went near her she embraced him. It was like being drawn to her as "steel to a magnet." The old woman (they said she was 122 years old) was none other than Hazrat Babajan, a Perfect Master. The magnet had held the steel. Merwan called on her every night and, after several months, one night...in January 1914 she kissed him on the forehead between the eyebrows. The kiss was the key: in a flash he found the infinite bliss of self-realisation. [9]

This was the first unusual experience of his life. During the first three days Merwan was unconscious of everybody and everything, although his body functioned normally. He lay in bed with vacant eyes and this worried Shireen. She was afraid her son was going mad and in panic, she rushed to Babajan. Babajan told her that Merwan was not mad but that he was intended to shake the world into wakefulness. He himself had described this later:

[9]   Baba explained the incident later: "At the time Babajan gave me the *nirvikalp* (inconceptual) experience of my own reality, the illusory physical, subtle and mental bodies — mind, worlds, and one and all created things — ceased to exist for me even as illusion. Then I began to see that only I and nothing else existed."

"When after the kiss from Babajan I knew that I was like the Ocean, I did not want to come back to the ordinary 'drop' consciousness from that Blissful State where I alone was. But despite my resistance the five Perfect Masters kept 'pulling me down' to ordinary consciousness for my destined manifestation as Avatar; and in this excruciating agony I went through this 'tussle.' I used to knock my forehead on a stone in my room at home, during the nine months before Upasni Maharaj brought me down to normal consciousness."

Meher Baba

Narayan Maharaj, one of the five Perfect Masters with whom Baba came in contact in 1915

Tajuddin Baba, one of the five Perfect Masters whom Baba contacted in the earlier years

Sai Baba, one of the five Perfect Masters, who addressed Meher Baba as 'Parvardigar' in December 1915

"Nine months after my self-realisation, I began to be somewhat conscious of my surroundings. Life returned to my vacant eyes. Although I would not sleep, I began to eat small quantities of food." (Merwan had not eaten food for nine months.)[10]

"Once I left Poona by rail for Raichur, (about 300 miles from Poona) but after travelling for only 34 miles I felt the urge to leave the train at Kedgaon. There for the first time I came in physical contact with Narayan Maharaj (one of the five Perfect Masters).

"Similarly, from time to time I was also drawn to see majzoobs like Banemiyan Baba at Aurangabad and Tipoo Baba at Bombay. Once I travelled as far north as Nagpur and saw Tajuddin Baba (another of the five Perfect Masters)."

In December 1915, Merwan was impelled to call on Sai Baba at Shirdi. He was coming in a procession. Merwan made his way through the large crowds and prostrated himself before him on the road. When he rose, Sai Baba looked at him and exclaimed, "Parvardigar" (God-Almighty-Sustainer).

Baba commented later: "I then felt drawn to walk to the nearby temple of Khandoba in which (Upasni) Maharaj was staying in seclusion. When I came near enough to him, Maharaj greeted me, so to speak, with a stone he threw at me with great force. It struck me on my forehead exactly where Babajan had kissed me, hitting with such force that it drew blood. The mark of that injury is still on my forehead. But that blow from Maharaj was the stroke of dnyan (Marefat of Haqiqat or divine knowledge)."

In 1916 Merwan took up a managerial assignment with a theatrical company on his mother's insistence to take up a job; but the company closed shutters two months later and Merwan too took over charge of his father's tea shop. He suffered intense spiritual agony and had a compulsive desire to do lowly work. He opened up a toddy shop in partnership with Buasahib, his friend and later on his disciple. Merwan worked for nearly eighteen hours each day in the toddy shop where he cleaned bottles, served customers and even swept the floor.

On this phase Baba commented: "That was the beginning of my present infinite suffering in illusion which I experienced simultaneously with my infinite bliss in reality. But it took me seven years of acute struggle under Maharaj's active guidance to return completely to, and become established in, normal human consciousness of the illusion of duality, while yet experiencing continuously my superconsciousness."

Merwan spent six months with Maharaj at Sakori from July to December 1921. "During those six months Maharaj and I used to sit near each other in a hut behind closed doors almost every night. On one such occasion, Maharaj folded his hands and said to me, 'Merwan, you are the Avatar and I salute you.' On another occasion, Maharaj told his disciples, 'I have given my authority to Merwanji. He is the holder of my key,' and later, 'This boy will move the world. Humanity at large will be benefitted at his hands.' "

Always wrapped in simple garments, Maharaj was one of the Perfect Masters who declared Merwan as the Avatar.

Merwan in 1921 when he spent six months with Upasni Maharaj at Sakori

The Early Days

In 1922 Merwan was 28. For about four months from January to May he stayed in a jhopdi (thatched hut) near Poona. Around him there were now a group of men who formed the nucleus of the mandali. They were his friends; they were also his disciples. Among them, one Sayyid Saheb started addressing Merwan as 'Meher Baba.' 'Baba' was an address of love, and of respect. The name would stay on all his life, and become for the world's millions, the most adorable four-letter word.

In these early days, the disciples around him had many strange experiences. It was the duty of one of the mandali members to keep watch outside the jhopdi when Baba retired at night. The vigil had to be sleepless. Once Behli Irani, one of the disciples, was on duty when he nodded off to sleep. When he woke up, he was shocked to find Baba's bed vacant. Behli was about to open the door when he saw weird figures moving about. He withdrew and sat down to weep and before long went to sleep. When he woke up again he found Baba asleep in bed.

Meher Baba in 1922

Meher Baba on the steps of the Manzil clad in a simple loin cloth

Meher Baba outside his jhopdi (hut) at Poona in 1922. Baba sang melodiously and played on several instruments as well.

[11] In March, 1922, Gulmai Kaikhushroo Irani, the wife of Khan Bahadur Kaikhushroo Irani, became the devotee of Meher Baba. Baba called her his 'spiritual mother' and her son Adi served Baba as his close disciple and secretary. Today Adi K. Irani disseminates Meher Baba's message from his office at King's Road, Ahmednagar, India.

On yet another occasion, one of the mandali was on duty with orders to sit outside the hut and not to permit any one to come near it. At about one o'clock, Baba called out to the guard, "Are you wide awake?" The guard replied that he was. Baba again said, "Whatever may happen, don't be frightened." With Baba's warning ringing in his ears the guard was startled to see two men in white robes approaching him. He called out to them and asked them who they were. Baba from inside the hut inquired what the matter was. The figures instantly vanished and Baba himself appeared.

It was during these months that Baba visited Kasbapeth every Thursday. His followers had grown in number and they gathered there to see him and hear him. There would also be arti in praise of Upasni Maharaj. Baba would join in with the others.[11]

A group photograph of Meher Baba with some of his earliest disciples. Baba is seen seated on the floor second from left.

Manzil-E-Meem

The first four months of 1922 passed. It was time for action. In May Baba came down to Bombay from Poona on foot. There were forty-five followers with him. In Bombay, he hired a bungalow on Main Road, Dadar, which he named 'Manzil-E-Meem' (house of the Master). It had fifteen rooms and on Baba's instructions, was kept unfurnished. Baba had made seven rules; the inhabitants of this house had to follow them to the letter.

1) Everyone should carefully follow the spiritual instructions given by the Master. [12]

2) Everyone should maintain, or break off, as ordered by the Master, any special connection with anybody.

3) Everyone should totally abstain from all intoxicants and from sexual intercourse.

4) None should partake of fish, meat or eggs under any circumstances.

5) All are bound to be in the Manzil from 7:00 p.m. to 7:00 a.m.

6) There should not be any lapses on the part of anyone in the performance of his duty.

7) Under no circumstances, except when ordered, should any member of the party leave the Master, even if the whole world turns against him.

One particular order concerned three members of the mandali. Whenever they were free from their particular duties, they had to sit near Baba in a particular order: Adi to sit on Baba's right, Ramjoo on his left and Ghani facing him. This strange order was in force for sometime; it was a disconcerting and enigmatic order, but it was scrupulously observed by all concerned at all times even at the most awkward places.

[12] Every morning Baba ordered his Hindu and Parsi disciples to visit their place of worship. His Muslim followers visited the mosque each Friday. The mandali members had at times to maintain a fast and feed beggars. Each mandali member had to work under Baba's instructions. This was the period of preparation and of intense activity. The slightest trace of disobedience or lack of discipline on the part of a mandali member would mean strict censure from Baba or even a severe beating.

An early photograph of Meher Baba with his first mandali at Manzil-e-Meem in 1922. Squatting l to r: Burjor, Adi K. Irani, Ramjoo Abdulla, Raghunath. Seated l to r: Behramji, Rustom K. Irani Meher Baba, Abdul Ghani, Gustadji. Standing: Babu Cyclewalla, H. J. Vajifdar, Sarosh Irani, Baidul, Adi Hansotia, Khodadad

It was evening. It was a Sunday. The tenth of September 1922. The mid-day meal was over and it was the hour of rest. Suddenly, a pigeon fluttered into the room. The pigeon was caught and taken to Baba. The bird was tired, it had no strength to fly. Baba lovingly nursed the sick bird. And he was anxious. He got up three times at night to see whether the pigeon had recovered.

In the morning Baba told his mandali that the pigeon had died. He asked them to have a last look at the remains of the bird — the bird had died in a queer posture, as if making a namaskar (obeisance with folded hands).

What did this signify? Baba had mentioned to his mandali sometime earlier that he would be receiving an important message from Hazrat Babajan. Now, after the pigeon died, Baba told them the meaning of the bird's visit. "This is the pigeon that has brought the important news from Babajan. The seriousness and gravity of the message can well be imagined that soon after delivering the heavy burden it dies." The bird was buried by Baba with a lot of care. A grave was prepared and a green sheet spread over the grave. Baba alone knew what the message said. With a few disciples he left for Ajmere. [13]

In the early 1922 days, Baba often gave talks, discussed many subjects with those around him. On October 4, 1922, Baba talked at length on the subject of 'Yoga and Mukti.' He said, "A Yogi even if he attains the highest yogic state in his study does not reach freedom (mukti) because there is still for him the sanskaras (impressions) bandhan (ties), to finish up with. Sanskaras mean impressions left behind while doing any good or bad action. Even a thought creates a sanskara. Talking, hearing, thinking, seeing, eating, sleeping, etc. in fact, even subtle movements cause sanskaras which have to be experienced without a single hitch with a mechanical precision unless removed away root and branch by a Master's grace. Our present existence and all the related experiences of pain and pleasure, virtue and sin are the results of the past sanskaras.

"The very breath we breathe, the eyelid we blink, the finger we lift is all due to the past impressions. Our present existence is the outcome of the unfoldment of our past subtle impressions in the gross forms. And again it is present gross actions that recreate impressions and so on. A good word or good action has its good result compressed in an impression (suppose in the form of circle) and a bad word or action likewise stores up a bad result in a similar circle form, that is, good actions in this life necessitate acquiring a happier state in the next formation and similarly a bad action in the present life brings about a bad result in the same way.

"Good actions bind a man with a golden chain and bad actions with iron and spiked chains. But the chain is there in either case, the man has not been set free! Yoga or other studies are good actions, and they give the person a better chance in the next birth. But it does not set him free or give mukti. Therefore, to have freedom, one must neither have virtue nor vice on one's credit or debit side, but it should be a clean slate, described in an Urdu couplet:

"I will neither go to heaven, nor will I go to hell,
I will only stand and gaze at the face of God."

and this is impossible to reach without the grace of the Guru. For a Master it is the work of a moment! The vast and almost infinite impressions of a person may be likened to a heap of dry grass which is impossible for a person to clean out. Even the

[13] Abdul Ghani Munsiff asked Baba on September 6, 1922 why there was a difference between his utterances and actions. Baba replied, "There are two kinds of Knowledge — the worldly knowledge or the knowledge relating to the material world and the divine knowledge which is acquired after becoming one with God. When dealing with matters relating to the material world, a person having become one with God reflects the actions and words of Divinity, although he does not utilise the divine knowledge within him. Hence the utterances and actions of such a person are invested with secrecy and grandeur. But this is often not understood by the worldly minds. For example, a ruby in the hands of a rustic will not be really appreciated by him, but the same ruby in the hands of a jeweller will have recognition and value. The person who has become one with God is able to make the best use of his worldly knowledge on the strength of his divine knowledge which he does not utilise, and therefore the difference between the utterances and actions of the ordinary human being and divine personalities."

13

process of cleaning out, without a Guru, that is through yoga etc., means contracting impressions again in different forms. But this heap of dry grass can be burnt in a moment by a lighted match, which only the Sadguru possesses. The Sadguru uses his matches but mostly for the members of his circle only and thus at the right moment brings them on his own level in less than a second. But even those who have no direct connection with a Sadguru can derive the greatest possible help merely by his contact and company.''

Enigmas pile up. The Master has his own ways. Not all is understandable, not all is explained. On the morning of February 4, 1923, Baba gave instructions that if he ever felt ill or lost consciousness, or if anything happened to his body, a doctor should not be brought even though he asked for one. Surprisingly, at about nine o'clock in the evening, he told the mandali not to sleep but to play 'Atya-patya' (the Indian form of rounders) in the courtyard. He himself joined the game. In the course of play, his toe was injured. He became seriously ill, vomited and was in agony. Then, as suddenly as it had happened, he got better and was soon fit as before. Meanwhile, two disciples had gone to call a bone-setter; when he came, Baba refused to see him.[14]

While at the Manzil, Ramjoo, one of the disciples, had once asked Baba what the stars were. Baba said: ''These are also circles like the planets and some of the latter are inhabited by people. They resemble this earth in culture, science, and in every material advancement, but spiritually this circle, the earth, is the most advanced. On some planets there are Masters in the flesh, but only on this earth are Sadgurus born. These circles appear to be at great distance from each other, but are really very close to one another. After realisation, Man beholds all of them (millions over millions) like small bubbles issuing forth from his own self, i.e. he experiences himself bigger than every-thing and every being, nay he finds he is the main source — the Maker of All. The material planes are different but the spiritual plane is one throughout.''

Enigmatic. Rhetorical. Mystical. Yes. And yet a witty con-versationalist. It was a joy to listen to him, to talk with him on spiritual and philosophical subjects. At the Manzil the food was simple, menu consisting of plain rice and dal for lunch and vegetables and bread for dinner. Sometimes the simplicity would be drastic, for some reason or other. As a result, the mandali had to subsist for long periods on one meal a day and some milkless tea.

[14] Dowlat (Shireen's elder sister) was an excellent cook and was equally fond of seeing her friends and relatives enjoy her food and she liked to see them eat plenty of it. In fact, if enough wasn't consumed to do justice to her cooking, she took it as an insult and remon-strated loudly. When Baba was at Manzil, she had taken along with her jars of pickle and lots of home-made eatables for him and the mandali. In those days Baba would flare up in sudden 'jalali' moods of anger that cleared up quickly but were profound while they lasted. All the gifts that Dowlat had brought were thrown away on the railway lines, and while expressing his anger, Baba picked up an earthen flower-pot and hurled it at her. Dowlat ran across the verandah and cleared with a bound the waist-high railing — an incredible feat at her age. The pot, however, crashed on the spot where Dowlat had been standing seconds before.

1923.1924. Till the end of the year Baba moved about with his mandali throughout India. He even visited Persia. During the course of this year he ate very irregularly, for months he took very little food and drink, and at times subsisted on just a few sips of tea, milk or soup. "I did not fast for the sake of fasting. I suffered and felt weak, just as any ordinary man who fasts." 15

15 In 1955 (November) Baba was asked why he had closed the Bombay ashram on the last day of March, 1923. His reply: "The money was finished. Therefore we went to Arangaon."

Meher Baba in Quetta in 1923

Meher Baba had tremendous personal magnetism and his eyes shone with an uncanny brilliance.

Meher Baba in Quetta, which he visited with his closest disciples in 1923

Meherabad

Despite all his tours, Baba would come back to Arangaon from time to time. Then in January 1925, he finally decided to settle down in the village permanently. About five miles from Ahmednagar, the village became his home, his seat. Gradually, people started calling the place Meherabad. The name came to stay. 16

At Meherabad, there is a well. An old well, it had been a source of water for the neighbouring villagers too. Near the well lies buried the Muslim Saint, Hazrat "Gilori Shah." It was in 1922 that the saint came over from Ahmednagar, drew a circle with his stick on the ground and told his disciples that was the spot where he wished to be buried. His followers could not understand why he should choose this lonely spot away from the

16 The story goes that while Baba was walking along the road leading to Arangaon, he saw a cluster of hutments and a solid stone one-room house. On inquiring, it was discovered that the property belonged to Baba's disciple, Kaikhusru Irani, Adi K. Irani's father.

Baba and his mandali decided to stay in the one-room house, which had earlier served as a post office. This was his first visit to Arangaon, which subsequently formed the nerve-centre of his universal work.

The unostentatious residential quarters of Meher Baba's mandali at Meherabad as it looked on September 15, 1935

[17] In 1967 I wrote to Meher Baba asking him whether I could, on my own, observe silence and meditate on him. Baba replied: "Do not observe prolonged silence or meditate. Do not serve yourself by doing so. You who lead a dedicated life in my cause have no need for such discipline. You are close to me and you are very dear to me. I know how you strive to be merged in my Love. I want you not to *strive* for this, but to allow your dear love to flow freely to me in its natural course. Know one most important thing in this spiritual live and that is that no amount of your striving to reach me could transport you to me. Simplest thing for you to do is to just love me in the most natural way, as a child would love his mother and carry out anything I *on my own* command you to do." Baba added later: "The world will know who I am when I break my silence and then *you* too will realize my infinite Love for you and my lovers."

Naosherwan

city. The saint replied: "You are little children. You would not understand if I told you what great importance this place will bear. Very soon after I pass away, a great Master will come and establish his abode here." The prophecy was fulfilled two years later.

In the course of the year, Meherabad, which was a small village, became a small town. Now it had a school, a hospital and dispensary and an ashram (hermitage) for lepers and the destitute. Hundreds of devotees and pilgrims came to Baba for his darshan (blessing). Also large multitudes of 'untouchables' would come for singing and prayers. Baba once reminisced: "Hundreds of people from the villages near Meherabad benefitted from the free hospitals and thousands utilised the dispensary provided for out-patients. Boys of all castes and creeds, including untouchables, lived, ate and intermingled freely.

"From dawn to dusk I would move about the place and take an active part in every phase including the cleaning of latrines. Each day I spent three to four hours bathing the school children. The mandali also had to grind grain for one to three hours each day, depending upon their assigned duties. I also shared in the daily grinding, for an hour or more."

The school was named after Hazrat Babajan. It provided free board, clothing and tuition to its inmates. Baba would look after the boys himself. From only twenty-two boys, the school grew to one hundred and fifty boys and girls.

One day, Baba, with the school teachers and the mandali, was washing and bathing some boys of the school. Some Brahmin visitors came for Baba's blessings and as they bowed to him, Baba said, "I am bathing untouchable boys. It is no use having darshan unless you are prepared to do the work I do." Shedding all their inhibitions, the Brahmins joined in. Baba was the compassionate father. Men are born to be free. They have no untouchability. Baba worked for the untouchables and the depressed classes. He loved them dearly, washed their feet, embraced them and gave them gifts. To them, and to all who came, Baba was the Saviour. [17]

16

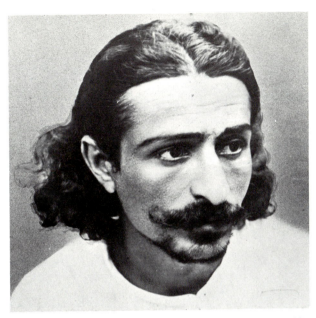

Meher Baba just before he started his silence on July 10, 1925

The Silence

On July 8, 1925, Baba called a meeting of his disciples. For about an hour, he explained what the duties of each would be. The time of his silence was approaching. The next day he summoned the parents and guardians of the boys in the school and explained what they should do to keep the school running. He would not speak, he said, because his spiritual task would be heavy. The time was close for the dropping of Babajan's body; also there were the turmoils, the wars and disasters which were coming to the world and to India in particular. He asked them not to lose heart. This period of crisis would end and there would follow a period of peace and tranquillity. [19]

Describing the beginning of this most wonderful event in the history of mankind, Faredoon Driver (Padri) narrates what happened on the night of July 9, 1925: "Before retiring at night at about 8:30 p.m. Baba talked and gave instructions to his mandali. At about 8:30 p.m. his words were, "I am now going. From tomorrow I will not speak for 1½ years. All of you must take care of your health; and remember, when any of you go out of the 'Makan' during the night to attend to your needs, always carry a lantern with you. Beware of snakes. I will do anything to help you in other difficulties, but I will not help

[18] On May 7, 1924, Baba sat in seclusion in an insect-proof room. Baba had declared that after entering the room he would cease to speak and convey his thoughts in writing only. But later in the evening Baba talked and said that he had suffered physically, not because of the fast, but because of intense spiritual work. This was probably the first indication of Baba's forthcoming silence.

[19] At the beginning of his silence, Baba wrote continually for hours daily the as yet unpublished book which Baba has declared as his Message to the world. Baba has stated that in this work he has revealed hitherto unknown spiritual secrets. Some of the "close ones" who lived with Baba have seen certain pages of the book and say that it has been written in several different languages simultaneously. One of Baba's American disciples has even made illustrations and charts for the book, all under Baba's direct supervision.

Meher Baba wearing a long flowing garment called 'sadra,' a simple, inexpensive garment made of soft cotton.

Meher Baba wrote the book in a small cupboard-like room constructed underneath the big wooden table during the year 1925 at Meherabad, Ahmednagar.

you if you are bitten by a snake.'' This was his final order. Baba left the 'makan' for his 'jhopdi' at Meherabad. The mandali too retired for the night. A few minutes later I took a lantern, stepped out about five to seven paces to relieve myself. Suddenly, by the light of the lantern I saw a snake in my path about twenty feet ahead and started shouting 'Snake,' 'Snake.' The mandali rushed out with sticks and killed the snake. Baba, hearing the commotion, returned and on being told of what had happened, once again enjoined about carrying a lantern and to beware of snakes. Finally he said (spoke): ''Now I am going,'' and went away. When we saw him on the morning of the tenth, he uttered no words.''

Baba's silence had begun. Silence. Not to speak. Not to use sound. But not isolation. His routine would go on. Baba said about this period later: ''At that time I communicated by writing on a slate and also, for more than a year, wrote for a number of hours daily on a work which remains unseen and unpublished to this day. I did most of my writing work in my small cupboard — like room constructed underneath the big wooden table which stands near the 'dhuni' (sacred fire-place). It was at this time (November 1925) that we began to light the dhuni each month.

''At certain fixed hours I saw visitors freely. Hundreds came daily for my darshan believing in my spiritual status, but most sought my blessings only for material benefit. On special occasions the stream of visitors would continue unbroken from morn to night and their numbers would run into thousands.''

During the Meherabad phase, many exciting events took place. Once a sadhu who wanted God-consciousness came to stay with Baba and agreed to remain under his instructions for a year. But not even a day had passed before the sadhu began to grumble about one thing or the other. Baba conveyed to the sadhu that God was not a 'cheap fruit' to be had for the asking, but demanded super-human patience! The sadhu went away.

On yet another occasion a yogi came to Baba for divine guidance. Baba asked him to stay at Meherabad and added the following peculiar words to his instructions. 'Matla, chatla, ghotla, vatla, satla, chotla, and potla' — the necessities for the life of a sadhu — a begging bowl, a water pot, a wooden rod, long braided hair and the bundle. For ten days the yogi went on with the instructions and on the tenth day asked Baba for leave. He complained that the food was not quite palatable!

Many a time visitors would come. They were men of intellect;

18

they came to test Baba's knowledge or to find proof of his spiritual status. On one occasion, a yogi, who had a large following and lived about 50 miles away from Ahmednagar, came to see Baba with the purpose of testing him. Baba usually did not see people of this sort, or answer their questions, but on this occasion he was in the mood and he asked the yogi to be brought to him. The yogi was given a slate to write his questions, and while he wrote, Baba also wrote on another slate, finishing his writing before the yogi had finished his. When the yogi's slate was handed to Baba, he put it aside without looking at it and handed his own slate to the yogi: it contained the answers to his questions. The yogi got up, prostrated himself and apologised profusely.

On February 27, 1926, Baba was given a telegram from his father. It was the news of the sudden death of Jamshed, Baba's eldest brother. Mani who was present at her brother's bed-side, narrates: "I can little remember my eldest brother Jamshed during the years of his life, but I well remember the time of his death, for I was there with him in Loni when he died at about the age of thirty-three and I was seven at that time. One thing I knew about him without a doubt and that was his intense love for Baba. At the time of his death he was with his foster parents and his wife in the village of Loni where my aunt and uncle lived for some time and where I was holidaying then. He too had been sent there by Baba for a few days. He seemed quite alright, and suddenly one night he had a pain in the heart. It was at midnight, and my aunt made him a cup of coffee and his wife rubbed some unguent on his chest. He had an intuition of his approaching death, for he bowed down at the feet of my uncle and aunt and asked their forgiveness for any omissions and commissions. He told them never to forget that Baba is God and told his wife never to leave Baba under any circumstances. Then he went back to bed. Just before dawn he died and with his last breath called out in a loud, clear voice, three times: "Baba, Baba, Baba."

When Baba asked the mandali if they felt any grief, they replied, "yes." Baba smiled. He said their grief was not genuine; it was hypocrisy and selfishness.

Someone said: "But from a worldly point of view, everyone must feel it."

"But why?" asked Baba. "That is where the mistake is made. It is all false."

19

"Was he not your brother, is he not dead?", remonstrated another.

Baba replied, "He was indeed my brother, but he is not dead. On the contrary, he is resting within myself."

"But how are we to know and appreciate that?", asked one mandali-member.

"From believing those who know the secrets of life and death" was Baba's final answer.

While yet on the subject of death, Baba said:

"Death is common to all. It is a necessary step forward towards life. The soul changes into a new abode, and thus death means no more than changing your coat. Or it may be compared with sleep. The difference between death and sleep is that after the first, one wakes up again in a new body, while in the latter one becomes conscious of the same body. Worldly people do not go into hysterics after one who goes to sleep at night because they expect to see him awake again. Then why not exercise the same indifference when he sleeps the sleep of death, since he is bound to wake up again sooner or later in a new body? Thus the selfishness of not being able to satisfy their minds in the absence of the sight of their dear ones makes them weep, not so much the death itself.

"After the death of a person, a cry is raised from all sides. 'My beloved father is dead.' 'The source of my life is gone.' 'The light of my eye is dimmed.' 'Where is my sweetheart?' 'My supporter has disappeared.' But in spite of the display of grief and pain, the 'my' and 'mine' remain uppermost rather than consideration of the welfare of the one who has passed away.

"The sword of death has been swinging right and left since the beginning of man's history. Every day I see hundreds and thousands of my brothers dying without feeling anything, and Jamshed's death is no exception to that. All admit that death is the unavoidable end and though the fact is universally acknowledged and experienced, yet at the time of its happening people start crying. That is either madness or weakness of mind! But Jamshed is not dead. If he were really dead, all should rejoice over it, since it means Real Life. Although you find me moving amongst you, playing with you and in fact doing all that a supposed living man does, I am really dead!

"I am living because I am dead! Die all of you in the real sense so that you may live ever after!"

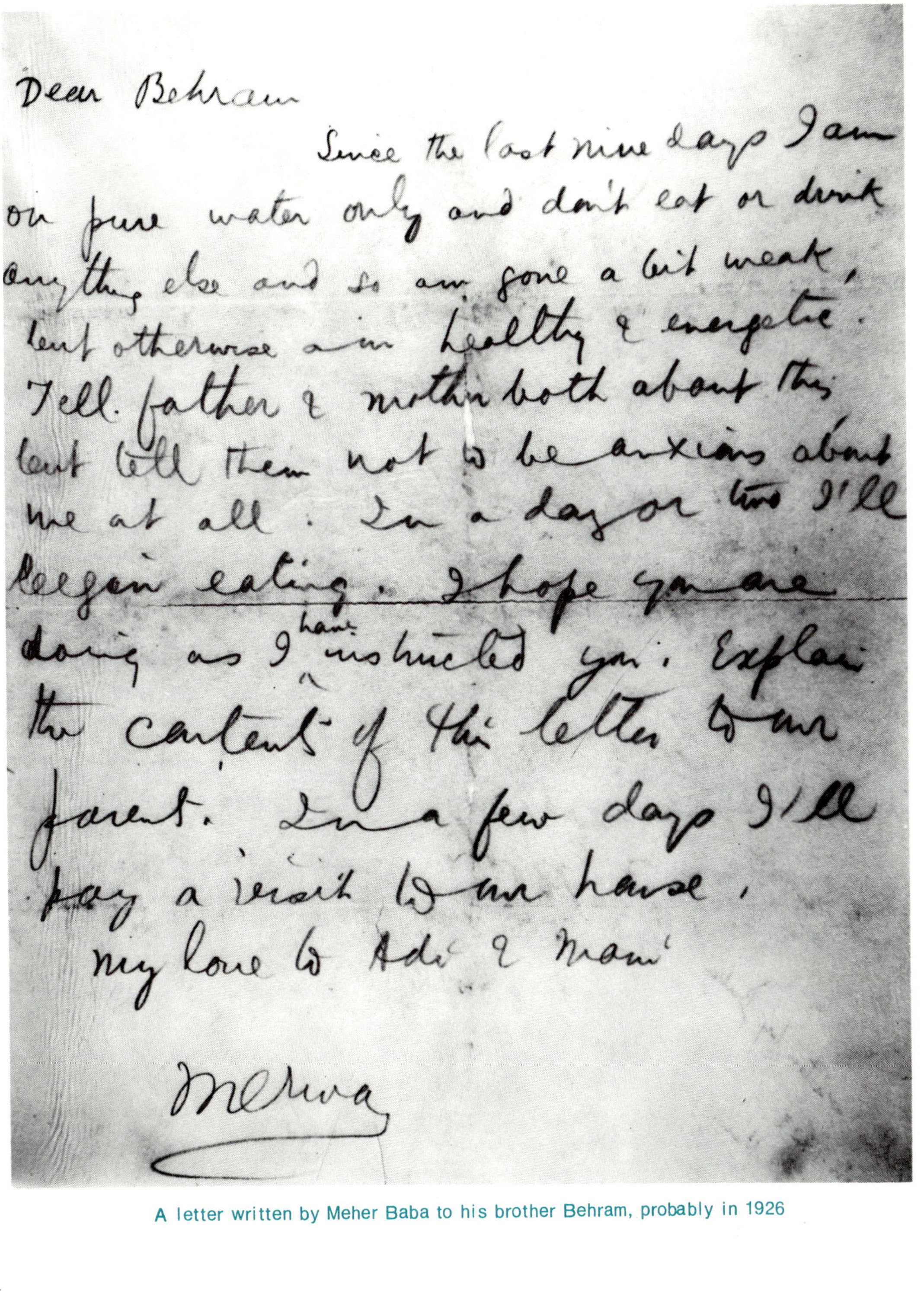

Dear Behram

Since the last nine days I am on pure water only and don't eat or drink anything else and so am gone a bit weak, but otherwise am healthy & energetic. Tell father & mother both about this but tell them not to be anxious about me at all. In a day or two I'll begin eating. I hope you are doing as I have instructed you. Explain the contents of this letter to our parents. In a few days I'll pay a visit to our house.

My love to Adi & Mani

Merwan

A letter written by Meher Baba to his brother Behram, probably in 1926

When Hazrat Babajan visited the school to see ''the place of my child'' it was a great event. But Baba indicated that this visit made it necessary for him to move the ashram from Meherabad to the village of Toka. The transference was completed within fifteen days. During the Toka stay Baba was very close to the boys and he did whatever they desired, at times undergoing immense suffering. During this period the boys were engaged in meditation as well, getting up early in the morning for that purpose.

He had not spoken for one and a half years. On January 1, 1927, he stopped writing as well and started using an alphabet board to convey what he had to say. On the first day of May the same year, Baba opened the Meher Ashram, at the outskirts of Arangaon. This was a school for boys to provide secular and spiritual education. This school was later shifted to Meherabad. It had started with ten boys: 4 Brahmins, 3 Mahars (untouchables) and 3 Marathas. In the later years, reminiscing on the school and its activities, Baba had commented: ''This school known as 'Meher Ashram' was started as a small day school for the boys of the adjoining village of Arangaon. After some time it was turned into a regular boarding school that housed more than a hundred boys. Efforts were made to collect them from various cities and different countries. One of the mandali was sent to England for that purpose. None came from the West, but a number of boys from Iran did join the Meher Ashram.'' [20]

On January 1, 1927, Meher Baba stopped writing and started using an alphabet board to convey his thoughts.

A B C D E F G H I
J K L M N O P Q R
S T U V W X Y Z + ?
1 2 3 4 5 6 7 8 9 0

"My first aim was to arrange for teaching the boys English through their various vernaculars, by standards set up in the University of Bombay. Having accomplished this, I began to spend all of my time, day and night, on the general welfare and spiritual upliftment of the boys.

"This was also the period when I carried out one of my longest continuous fasts, which lasted five and one half months (November, 1927 – April, 1928). Once during this period I took nothing but a few sips of water for more than twenty-eight days. The remainder of the time I lived on cocoa in milk taken once in twenty-four hours."

Those who had come to live with Baba had changed totally, as if their lives had metamorphosised. They had strange experiences, both internal and external. Of special significance is an incident which occurred during the Ashram days, herein adapted from Ramjoo Abdulla's account in his book, 'Sobs and Throbs':

Meher Baba with the boys of the Prem Ashram in 1927. Ali can be seen in the foreground.

On January 1, 1928, the fifty-second day of Baba's fasting and the twelfth of his self-imposed confinement, a majority of the boys began to break into tears at different times throughout the day.

For about an hour between seven and eight in the evening, this awesome phenomenon held the onlookers spellbound. The tumult could be heard a quarter of a mile away from the ashram.

Among all the boys, the weeping of one in particular, Aga Ali, was most pathetic. On January 28, Baba openly declared Ali to be quite ready with sufficient love to enable him to be taken away from the domain of the "bound" to the region of the "free" but for a final touch from Baba!

On the following day Ali went into uncontrollable sobbing. The sobs were heart-rending and Ali's whole frame shook. It was nearly 9:30 at night and this piquant drama had continued for nearly three hours. Ali seemed beyond the capability of controlling his sobs. But only a few minutes later Baba gathered Ali in his arms, patted his head, imprinted a kiss on his forehead and placed his head on the boy's heaving bosom for a few minutes. Ali became as calm as a mill pond. The onlookers soon realised that Ali would not open his eyes, and when his eye-lids were pulled up, the iris was found turned inward.

Several questions were repeatedly put to him but no reply was received. After some time, to a question, "How are you, Aga Ali," he replied "Khush" (happy). "What do you see?" "Baba." "Where?" "Everywhere." [21]

The same year the school was divided into two sections, the general section where normal studies went on, and the 'Prem Ashram,' a special section of the school where boys spent their time in meditation. Baba continued to give most of his time and attention to the Prem Ashram boys. To teach humility, Baba cleaned the boys' latrines with his own hands for a period of one month.

In September of 1929 Baba paid a second visit to Persia. He visited several places, and in Yezd, where he stayed for four days, the entire town flocked to him. He met people individually and in groups. Iran was passing through a transitional phase in history. Those who had come to meet Baba thought his visit was a good omen: maybe this would bring their country's redemption.

The year 1930 was spent by Baba mainly in touring large areas of India. He would travel by every conceivable mode, irrespective of discomfort.

[21] In May, 1928, Baba with his mandali was travelling in a car from Bombay to Meherabad. The car, a sturdy Hudson Super Six, managed to climb the Bhor Ghat, between Campoli and Khandala, but about half-way the car began to roll back. All attempts of the driver to stop the car failed, for even the brakes were out of order. The vehicle was heading for a deep chasm. Baba leaned on one side of the car, pressed it down with his hand and it came to an instant halt! Many miraculous incidents have been attributed to Baba and he persistently denied them. He always attributed such incidents to the faith and love of his disciples.

Meher Baba seen in the compound of Lower Meherabad probably in the year 1927

An early photograph of Meher Baba in 1927 at Meherabad wearing his old patched coat and tattered sandals

Slim, lithe, with large luminous eyes marking his striking personality, Meher Baba was always agile and active. He is seen here sitting against Hazrat Babajan School building, probably in the year 1927.

Meher Baba with the entire Ashram at Toka in 1928. The group is flanked by some of his earliest western disciples.

Meher Baba at Toka in 1928 dressed as a Maharashtrian peasant

Meher Baba with some members of his mandali during a boat ride on the lake near Toka in 1928

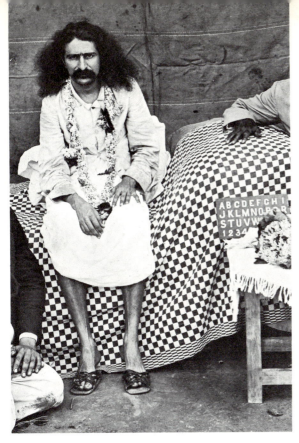

Meher Baba at Bijapur in 1930

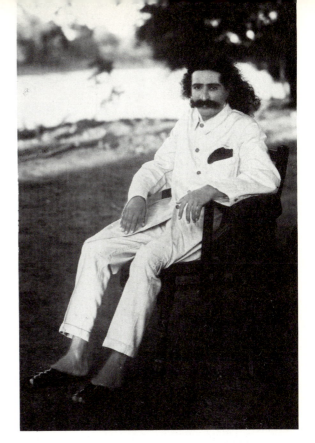

Meher Baba in 1929 dressed in a Parsi long coat and trousers

Visits to the West

Meher Baba, had by now spent 15 years in India, one and a half decades spent in preparing his eastern group of disciples. It was time to go to the West, the other civilisation. He came to the West for the first time in 1931. There he laid the foundation of the new phase for his work when he gathered around him an intimate group of western disciples.

In 1927 Baba had sent Rustom Irani, a close disciple, to England to bring back a few English boys so that the West might be represented in the school. While in England, Rustom met an Englishman named Meredith Starr. Shortly after this meeting Rustom returned to India without any English boys, but Meredith came to India and stayed with Baba in his Ashram in Toka for six months. He returned to England after a happy stay with Baba.

Meher Baba during his first visit to England in 1931 in the house of Mrs. Davy at Russell Road

22 Mahatma Gandhi had several meetings with Meher Baba, on board ship as well as at the Knightsbridge Hotel at London and the Congress House at Bombay. Gandhi discussed with Baba several political and social problems and Baba readily suggested remedial measures. During their meeting in Bombay in the forties, Gandhi declared, placing his hand in Baba's, that on completion of his political activities he would join Meher Baba's ashram and translate and disseminate Baba's Message to the world. Gandhi's philosophy of non-violence is largely influenced by Meher Baba.

On his return Meredith founded a retreat in anticipation of Meher Baba's visit.

On July 17, 1931, Baba sent a cable from Karachi saying that he would go to England. During August, his sailing was repeatedly postponed. Then on September 4, 1931, Baba sailed for England with three of his disciples. He had made a prophecy nine years earlier that he and Mahatma Gandhi would meet on the boat on his first trip to the West. Now, when Baba's party boarded the S. S. Rajputana, they discovered that Gandhi was also a passenger. Later, Gandhi's secretary relayed the message that the Mahatma would like to meet Baba. A meeting was arranged in Baba's cabin where they talked about spiritual matters. During the voyage Gandhi read a chapter of 'Creation' from Baba's hitherto unpublished book. Gandhi was most impressed by what he read. They met several times on the boat as well as in England and Bombay. **22**

While in London, many people came to see Baba and many reporters wrote sensational copy. But the important meetings were with those men and women who were destined to become his first Western disciples. Margaret Craske, who had danced with with the Diaghilev Ballet and later had her own dancing school in London, gives her impressions of her first meeting with Baba:

"As I entered the room I was completely won over by the love which seemed to permeate his whole personality. The whole time was invested with a dream-like quality of pure love, timelessness and great beauty. It was as if the curtain had been drawn aside and we were privileged to know and feel from our hearts who Baba is."

Another Englishman, Quentin Todd said of his first meeting, "I was so engrossed in looking at this wonderful man for the first time that everything else faded away. What impressed me most was his rather wild quality, as of something untamed, and his truly remarkable eyes. He smiled and motioned me to sit beside him. He took my hand and from time to time patted my shoulder. We sat for several minutes in silence and I was aware of a great feeling of love and peace emanating from him; also a curious feeling of recognition came to me, as if I had found a long lost friend."

And yet another who was drawn to Meher Baba was Delia de Leon who says, "I was stunned with the wonder and beauty of him. I had seen his face before in my dreams; the eyes were startling in their beauty; the face seemed of luminous honey colour, framed by a halo of long, dark hair. His hands were most noticeable; they were strong, slim and sensitive.... Everyone and everything faded from my mind except Baba. He alone seemed real — the Perfect Human Being. From that moment I gave my life into his keeping and I knew that my spiritual search was at an end."

Of the scores of interviews that Baba gave while in London, two instances are quoted here. A woman asked Baba how she could develop the realisation of the divine within her soul. Baba answered: "True spirituality can be attained not by the intellect, but by heart and feeling — by inner experience. I might explain for hours, but that would be as nothing compared to one second of my internal help. Do one thing. Every night, just before retiring, think for a moment: 'The infinite God is within me, and I am part of the infinite.' This will strengthen your inner contact with me."

Someone asked Baba why when he was the Christ did everyone not accept him. To this Baba replied: "It is the human form which I must take that stands in the way of their recognition. Jesus was not acknowledged in his time, even by some of his own intimate and immediate companions, such as Judas. Though none of you understand me externally in my physical form, I am within you — within everybody — as the Real, Infinite Christ."

Meher Baba talking to newsmen of *S. S. Bremen* at New York Pier on May 19, 1932

During his stay at London he went to a Promenade Concert, to several theatres, to the Zoological Gardens, to several museums and to the Unknown Warriors' grave at Westminister Abbey. While he was staying at Kensington, London, in the house of the Davys, on a certain day, he sent for Mrs. Davy and asked her if there was anything he could do. She replied shyly, "We have a home for old folks over eighty and I would like you to visit them, but you have no time." It was lunch time then. Surprisingly, Baba sent for his secretary, told Miss Kitty Davy to order a taxi at once and set off for the home.

Later in the day, Mrs. Davy asked Baba, "How can I understand and love you?" Baba replied, "When you pray, have my picture before you." "I have always the picture of Christ," she said. "Keep looking at the Christ's picture. It is the same," replied Baba.

From England Baba went to Constantinople, then to Milan and Genoa whence he sailed to America for New York. His U. S. stay was for one month, three weeks in Harmon on the Hudson River

During Baba's stay at Harmon-on-the-Hudson, N. Y., Harry Barnhart, a mind-reader, tried to probe into Baba's mind. To his utter amazement he found that he could read nothing. He felt that Baba's mind was an absolute blank and he explained later, ''Yet all through the interview I was knowing that Baba was reading every thought and feeling!'' When Harry's remarks were mentioned to Baba, he answered: ''I have no mind in the customary sense of the word — only a universal mind; which to read, requires a universal mind.''

and one week in New York City. [23] He returned to India in early 1932, but soon thereafter, on March 24 of the same year, he left India for his first world tour. He again visited England where he gave his message to the West. Here is an extract:

''I am not come to establish any cult, society or organization — nor to establish a new religion. The Religion I shall give teaches the knowledge of the One behind the many. The Book which I shall make people read is the book of the heart, which holds the key to the mystery of life. As for ritual, I shall teach humanity to discriminate, express, and live rather than observe it. I shall bring about a blending of the head and the heart. Societies and organizations have never succeeded in bringing truth nearer. Realisation of Truth is solely the concern of the individual.''

The London dailies hailed Meher Baba as a 'Messiah' and called him Gandhi's spiritual adviser. The composite picture shows Meher Baba at Meherabad, India in 1926 (above), Devonshire Retreat and a section of its inmates (below), Baba's seclusion cell at Panchagani (inset).

Meher Baba at the Devonshire Retreat, England in 1932

Meher Baba addressing his lovers at the Devonshire Retreat, England, in 1932. His Indian disciples can also be seen in the picture.

The darshan during his London stay would start at 9:00 in the morning. Every day at least 100 people would come to see Baba. Baba spent an entire day at Kew Gardens, a few hours at the British Museum, an afternoon on different underground railways and visited a few theatres. People were media; he had to work through people. On this particular visit Baba was extensively interviewed by all leading newspapers of London; he also gave personal interviews. [24]

Baba continued his journey to Paris and further to Lugano [25] arriving in New York amidst a blare of publicity. Here Baba gave this message:

"America has tremendous energy, but most of this energy is misdirected. I intend to divert it into spiritual and creative channels.

"My work will arouse great enthusiasm and a certain amount of opposition — that is inevitable. But spiritual work is strengthened by opposition, and so it will be with mine. It is like shooting an arrow from a bow — the more you pull the bow-string towards you, the swifter the arrow speeds to its goal."

[24] "He has a gentle, affectionate manner and welcomed me with a graceful inclination. His large, black eyes are very observant, lit up with a pleasant expression as his thin brown finger moved swiftly across the alphabet board on his knee."

Daily Mirror
April 13, 1932

"Baba conveyed to me the impression of intelligence and power, and a curious feeling as though all one's thoughts were being read almost before one had thought them."

Daily Mirror
April 21, 1932

[25] While Meher Baba was away to the West, Sheriar died on April 30, 1932 at the age of seventy-nine.

Meher Baba at the Eiffel Tower, France,
with his Eastern and Western disciples

At Hollywood in the Paramount studios Baba was received by some of the directors and shown the place of work. Baba attended a reception given in his honour by Mary Pickford and Douglas Fairbanks and on another day a reception of about a thousand film celebrities, where Baba gave a message, a part of which is reproduced here: "The root of all our difficulties, individual and social, is self-interest.... But the elimination of self-interest, even granting a sincere desire on the part of the individual to accomplish it, is not so easy, and is never completely achieved except by the aid of the Perfect Master. For self-interest springs from a false idea of the true nature of the self, and this idea must be eradicated and the Truth experienced, before the elimination of self-interest is possible."

During his visit to Hollywood in 1932 Meher Baba met a number of people connected with the film world. Here he is seen with Tallulah Bankhead. She had several private interviews with Meher Baba.

A profile of Meher Baba in Los Angeles in 1932

Meher Baba reading the *Los Angeles Times* issue dated 1932

In the spring of 1932, Meher Baba visited Sand Dunes, a place 200 miles north of Hollywood where he met a number of seekers.

In 1932 Meher Baba visited Nanking, China.
L to r : Vishnu, Adi S. Irani, Pendu, Meher
Baba, Kaka Baria, F. H. Dadachanji and
Jal S. Irani

Meher Baba photographed near the Sphinx in
Egypt

From America Baba sailed for China and made a second visit
to Europe, a trip to Egypt and returned to Bombay. An important
feature of this trip was a visit to Assisi where Baba stayed in a
special cave connected with St. Francis. Here he did his
universal work in seclusion.

In the winter of 1932, Baba sent certain of his disciples to
travel through Germany, Austria, Italy and Hungary, and some to
China and America, to carry forth his message of love and peace.
Earlier in the same year he had sent two disciples to Australia
and New Zealand on a similar mission. In mid-November he
sailed for Europe and before his departure sent a message to
India in which he stated that ''India is a spiritual country. It
possesses the most fortunate and unique position in the world of
being the land of saints and spiritual masters, since ages.
Therefore the spiritual atmosphere of India must be kept up even
at the cost of being in bondage and materially unhappy.... It is
only after experiencing bondage and misery that the true value of
freedom and happiness is really appreciated.... The world will
soon realize that neither cults, creeds, dogmas, religions,
ceremonies, lectures, and sermons, on the one hand, nor, on the
other hand, ardent seeking for material welfare or physical
pleasures, can ever bring about real happiness — but that only
selfless love and universal brotherhood can do it.''

Baba returned to India after a second visit to Egypt and a
brief stay in Ceylon. In Ceylon he went into seclusion for some
time in a temple in the hills.

Meher Baba with his Eastern and Western
lovers on the way to Kashmir in 1933. L to r
seated: Ramjoo, Norina, Minta and Mabel.
Standing: Meher Baba, Elizabeth, Vivienne,
Delia, Kitty, Margaret, Kaka, Christine and
Ghani

Meher Baba at Agra in 1933. He travelled extensively and met several spiritual contacts throughout the years of his universal work.

Meher Baba in Venice in 1932 with Kaka and Adi K. Irani

Meher Baba in Venice in 1932. Seated l to r: Quentin Todd and Mabel Ryan. Standing l to r: Enid Corfe, Kitty Davy, Kaka Baria, Meher Baba, Delia De Leon F. H. Dadachanji, Herbert Davy, Minta and Margaret Craske

Meher Baba at Portofino in 1932, with Quentin Todd (*above*) and Herbert Davy

On his fifth visit to the West in 1933 Baba visited Rome and Portofino. He returned to India in July and made a sixth visit to Europe in September of the same year. He stayed in London for thirteen days and left for Spain and, after nearly a month, returned to India.

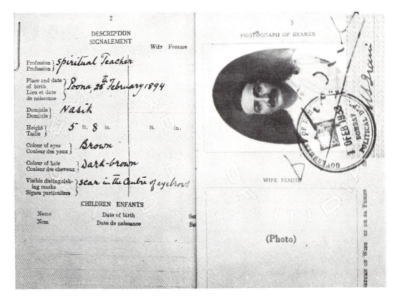

The passport shows Meher Baba's personal description and a photograph with his signature. It was made before Meher Baba's fifth visit to the West in 1933 when he visited Rome and Portofino.

Baba's seventh visit to the West was in the summer of 1934 when he visited Paris, London and Zurich, where he stayed for six days. During his stay in London, Baba met a number of people. In the course of an interview Baba was questioned on his ways of working. Baba replied, "There are three principal ways in which I work: 1) individually, 2) collectively (for crowds and masses), and 3) universally.

"When I work individually, it's with persons a) who are with me, b) who are away from me, and c) who are connected with me.

"In some cases, I work through their material downfall; in some cases through their material welfare, in some cases I deliberately bring about material downfall, but always having in the background their spiritual upliftment at heart. In some cases, I use them as 'mediums' to efface their own 'mayavic' qualities for their own salvation and that is where I am misunderstood. But I do not mind it. I know why I do it. That is sufficient; because, when carried to the extreme, love and hatred both have the same results. For example, A loves me extremely. It means he thinks

Three Photographs at left (top to bottom):
Meher Baba at Naples in 1933 with Jal, Vishnu, Kaka and Adi, Jr.
Baba in Egypt with members of a local family in 1933
Baba with Quentin Todd on his way to Egypt in the same year

continually of nothing else but me and is perfectly lost in me. B is extremely against me, i.e. hates me, but always thinks of me and is lost in me though with antagonistic feelings....I always use the medium of thoughts...it depends upon the qualities that readily respond to the push.

"When I work collectively, which is generally in theatres, picture houses, sporting grounds and in games, etc., where people collect and concentrate on a particular object, it is easy for me to have my spiritual effect on their minds collectively.

"When I work universally — through agents — my mind being universal, it is linked up with every individual mind.... Even with advanced minds, who are my agents, and so in every part of the world, I am present and working through agents. That is why at times a) while speaking to one person, my mind is working elsewhere. People have seen and marked me stopping suddenly in the midst of conversation as if absent and always away from the spot and engrossed in something else.

"b) At nights, on many occasions, I make some of my devotees sit beside me and press the soles of my feet (i.e., to have a physical touch). c) Sometimes my personal attendant abruptly sits up in his bed at night, noticing some signs or flash of light, which makes him nervous. At such times, there is special working which pertains to bodiless 'spirits' only, who are entering the Path of Evolution. There are scores of such 'spirits' but whatever their stage of advancement, they hope to take form again, because the ultimate goal of every soul is to be one with the Infinite, and that is only possible in human form.... This is, in short, how I work."

During his stay in Switzerland, Baba spent a day on the mountain, Fallenfluh. He sat in a hollow on the northern side of the mountain for two hours, no one being allowed to go near him.

In the later months of 1934 and in early 1935, Baba made his eighth visit to Europe and his second world tour when he again visited London. He was to continue his journey to America, and then on to Hollywood for Vancouver, to return to India via Hong Kong and Colombo, by the land route. [26]

In early 1936 Baba started a new phase of his work. Along with a few selected members of the mandali, Baba set off for Rahuri, a town 23 miles from Meherabad where he gathered together a number of mad people and masts (the spiritually intoxicated), upon whom he waited with his own hands. He bathed them, fed them, clothed them, and carefully looked after

[26] "When will you break your vow of silence?
BABA: There is no vow of silence. My twelve years of silence is no ascetic vow, but a period of working in silence for the spiritual upheaval preceding the manifestation of my universal work. But I shall speak. As the surgeon's knife cuts the matured cataract and restores sight, so when the world is ripe my message shall restore the drooping spirit of the world."

Associated Press of India
Bombay
November 23, 1936

Meher Baba in Hollywood in 1935. During his stay there he had a very busy schedule wherein he held discussions and talks with those who handled the work of producing a spiritual film which would project his message to humanity on the screen. Although the project never materialised, a large number of sincere seekers were drawn to Meher Baba.

Meher Baba in Hollywood in 1934. First row, l to r: Jeanne Adriel, Nonny Gayley, Ruano Bogislav. Second row, l to r: Jal S. Irani, Minta Toledano, Meher Baba, Norina Matchabelli, Nadine Tolstoy, Elizabeth Patterson and Rano Gayley

A rare photograph of Meher Baba at Zurich in July 1934 cycling on the lawn of Hedi Mertin's home

Meher Baba at Marseilles in July 1934. L to r: Ruano Borgislav, Delia De Leon, Rano Gayley, Meher Baba, Elizabeth Patterson, Nonny Gayley, Kaka Baria and Norina Matchabelli

Meher Baba surrounded with children during his visit to Zurich in 1934

all their needs. These seemingly strange human "derelicts" were accommodated in special huts and for Baba, the work of looking after these people was extremely exacting. Despite their filthy physical conditions they were spiritually ripe men and Baba chose to do his universal work through them. Work at Rahuri lasted for eight months, until the end of April 1937. There, temporary buildings had been erected along with a hut for Baba and a dispensary where sick people from all over the countryside were treated free of cost.

The men who arrived at the ashram were always restless and at times belligerent; some wanted to leave at once. But after Baba had given them a bath with his own hands, they became composed and settled down at the ashram. During this period, Baba rose at 4:00 a.m. each day and retired at midnight. He served the mad, cleaned out their latrines, bathed them, sat with some of them in seclusion, and, in fact, fulfilled their every whim and fancy. They were given whatever they asked for and were always very well-fed.

Baba, who did much of his work through the masts, describes them as "those who become permanently unconscious in part or whole of their physical bodies, actions, and surroundings, due to their absorption in their intense love and longing for God. My love for the masts is similar in many ways to that shown by a mother who continues to look lovingly after her children regardless of their behaviour."

The men Baba calls masts are not defective in the physiological sense, but they are physically unbalanced. They suffer from nothing that can be called a disease. They are in a state of mental and physical disorder because their minds are overcome by strong spiritual energies overpowering them, forcing them to renounce the world, normal human habits and customs, and civilized society, and to live in dirty surroundings. Baba called them 'God-intoxicated souls.' Baba said that, "they are overcome by an agonising love for God and are drowned in their ecstasy; only love can reach them." **27**

The work of contacting the masts, taking care of them, looking after them, often meant long journeys, sometimes by train, on foot, riding on camels, mules and asses, in bullock carts and tongas, travelling over sand, through jungles, over mountains and most times without food or sleep.

Baba plunged himself into all the hardships that went with his work and his mandali were always at hand to lend their

Meher Baba with his first mast contact in 1929. It was later that he contacted a very large number of masts and formed mast ashrams where he worked with them.

27 Dhondibua, the mast, when given anything for his material needs, would refuse it saying "I cannot bear comfort!" He would remain naked in all weather, be it in the blazing sun or piercing cold; and when a shirt or blanket was given to him by someone, he would gently but firmly reject the gift explaining that comfort did not agree with him. He would sometimes be seen rolling in the dust. Baba said, "This was from the agony of love for God that the genuine masts have. You cannot have the slightest idea of what such love means — it is an unbelievable agony that continually burns the lover, so that he is but a living fire! This love is a gift from God, whereas God-realisation is attained only by the Grace of the Perfect Master. Even these real men of God, the masts, do not all gain God-realisation — as a matter of fact, out of very many only one gets it!"

physical support. This work with the masts continued month after month, year after year, with periods of recuperation at Meherabad and intervals of prolonged fasting and seclusion.

Although Baba had started contacting the God-mad in 1915, his regular work with the masts started only in 1938. The series of mast-tours lasted for nearly nine years covering over 75,000 miles. On these tours, Baba's main object was to contact masts of every kind in all parts of India; he very seldom asked the masts to be brought to him; he almost always went to them. Besides the masts, Baba sought out sadhus and faqirs who had renounced the world and yearned for God-consciousness; but masts remained his main concern.

Between 1939 and 1947, Baba planned and supervised seven main mast ashrams and these were maintained at different places such as Ajmer, Jabalpur, Bangalore, Meherabad, Ranchi, Mahabaleshwar and Satara.

Some of the masts at Meher Baba's Rahuri ashram in 1937

Meher Baba often travelled incognito. Here he is seen in an Arab costume some time around 1936.

(Right) Meher Baba answering questions at Rahuri in 1936 to Dr. Abdul Ghani Munsiff

October, 1936 The mast work came to a temporary halt. Baba's ninth visit to the West. London, Zurich, Paris. His message to the West had taken roots. Now it was time for disciples to come and work and live with him. They would be the initiates. The new Ashram at Nasik was ready now. Baba returned in the end of November. In December over twenty disciples came from England and America. To the group that came, Baba indicated: "Everyone of you has to help in my work according to your individual capacity; and the extent to which you will remain in the world will be determined by the kind of work which you are destined to perform. I will teach you how to move in the world yet be at all times in inward communication with me as the Infinite Being.... As part of your training you will have to experience both the comforts of Nasik and the discomforts of Meherabad."28

In 1937 a large number of Meher Baba's Western lovers came to India for spiritual learning under his guidance. The group photo shows Meher Baba with his Eastern and Western disciples at Meherabad.

28

Letter dated April, 1937, NASIK:

I am writing to you from India. Destiny brought me here — and this destiny is none else but the Will and Grace of Shri Meher Baba.

You can imagine how I felt when I received definite news from Baba, that I am included in the group of Westerners who have been called to come in this "Meher Retreat," in Nasik. Here we receive more intensive training under the personal guidance of the Master, to share later in his great universal work.

I know you will understand how much happiness it means to be with the Beloved Master in his home. What a source of great spiritual learning and great spiritual experiences; here we live under his vigilant, all-knowing guidance in the very heart of what is the highest and the purest in this world, surrounded by Love, guided by Love. To him we can bring our deepest sores and problems, to him our hearts are open! He is that Divine Friend who heals all hearts by giving Light and Love with tender patient care as our dearest Mother and Father. In short, with him we are in constant Presence and Love of Christ. Being so close to him we have all the accessible opportunities to witness the unique manifestation of his work.

Nadine Tolstoy

1937 Nasik Birthday Party

29 One of the most memorable experiences of our stay in India was Baba's birthday celebration, the preparations for which began shortly after our arrival in December. Forty days before the birthday a fast began in which we all shared. The fifteen of us in turn joined Baba in a one-day fast of two cups of tea and two cups of milk. Again, we all participated as he fasted without even water for twenty hours of the day....

Thousands of yards of cloth had been purchased, together with tons of rice and lentils to be made into birthday packages for the poor. The Westerners worked at all spare moments tying up these bundles of food, until finally a pyramid of packages, twelve feet high, arose in the midst of the garden. The Ashram hummed with activity and by the fifteenth of February the preparations were completed....

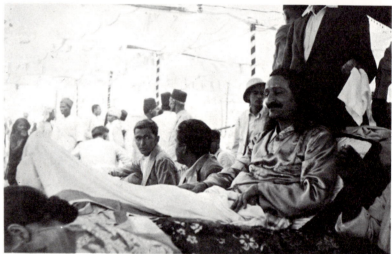

During the birthday celebrations ten thousand men, women and children in all stages of poverty and physical need filed past the platform, holding out emaciated hands for food and bundle. Here and there one could see indications in their eyes of a hunger which transcended the physical, as they would come before Baba, bowing their heads to his feet, then looking up into his eyes for a brief moment. As Baba would touch their feet with his sensitive hand, one wondered what measure of his divine love they were able to receive....

Reprinted from the AVATAR
by Jean Adriel
© 1947 by Jean Adriel

Meher Baba at Trimbak in 1937

(Above) Meher Baba's Western women disciples with some of his Eastern women disciples at lower Meherabad in 1937. L to r: Margaret Craske, Freinymasi, Ruano Borgislav, Daulatmai, Kitty Davy, Meher Baba, Norina Matchabelli, Nadine Tolstoy and Delia De Leon

(Below) Meher Baba's Ashram in Nasik in 1937 was built for Westerners with all western amenities. While the period of training was rigorous, all the personal comforts of the Westerners were looked after.

After a seven months training period at the Nasik Retreat,[29] the group of Westerners were asked by Baba to return and prepare for his visit to France, where he would bring a large number of his Eastern mandali including one of his chosen masts, Mohammed. On July 31, 1937 Baba sailed for Cannes on the French Riviera. It was the first time that he brought with his party six of his close women disciples to the West. During his stay many Europeans were given an opportunity for an interview with Baba.[30]

During this period Baba and some of his Eastern and Western disciples went by motor to Paris where they were guests in the

Meher Baba with Mohammad in 1937

[30]"Service is not any service. To be effective there must be no lingering idea that one is free to yield service or refuse it. One must feel that one is not master of the body — which is the Gurus', and exists merely to render him service."

—Meher Baba
Cannes, 1937

During his visit to Cannes in 1937 Baba gave several private interviews. Here he is seen conversing with Consuelo Sides. She and her husband Alfredo were Baba's hosts in Paris in the same year.

apartment of Alfredo and Consuelo Sides overlooking the Seine River. The Paris World Fair was going at that time and Baba encircled it by car without going inside the Fairgrounds. He took his party up the Eiffel Tower. After two days they returned to Cannes. In November 1937, Baba returned to India on the S. S. Circassia.

Meher Baba with his disciples at Capo-di-Monte, Cannes, in 1937

Meher Baba on board the ship *S. S. Circassia* in November 1937 on his way to India from Cannes

He returned to India with three of the women disciples from the West; they were joined by some others later. To give up the freedom they had become accustomed to, to live together without claiming too rigid privacy, to move always within bounds, and above everything else, to do the tasks given by Baba that needed complete concentration — for the Westerners it was an entirely new experience. Conflicts would arise, as is natural where personalities are strong, but Baba permitted these discords to develop, confronted those involved in the situation, made them analyse their problems and without compromise or sacrifice brought them together in love. **31**

Meher Baba at Meherabad in 1937 with his women mandali

31 When Meher Baba permitted women to join his ashram, Daulatmai and her daughter Mehera were among the first to come. Baba told them that they would have to live a very strict and secluded life, wear simple clothes and work hard. Above all they had to obey his orders implicitly.

Mehera J. Irani, Baba's chief woman disciple, narrates her first encounter with Babajan. One afternoon during her school recess, her friend Zeena told her: "Let's go to Babajan. She is a great person and can give you anything you ask for." They found Babajan sitting by the roadside outside the wall of the Convent. Mehera shyly approached Babajan, who asked her, "What is it, my child?" Mehera, without any forethought of what she would say, blurted out, "Babajan, I would like to have a nice white horse." Babajan looked at her, smiled and turning her head sidewards gazed intently up at the sky. Then nodding her head she said, "Very beautiful and fine. All the world will look on him in admiration and love." In reality, Hazarat Babajan had referred to "the White Horse Avatar," which in Hindu mythology is termed as Horse-head, a form assumed by Vishnu to recover the Vedas when they were stolen. Mehera later joined Meher Baba's ashram in fulfilment of her desire and recognition of Babajan's boon. Baba once said, "Mehera is to me as Radha was to Krishna."

Meher Baba at Meherabad in 1938 conversing on his alphabet board

Meher Baba at Panchagani in 1938 with Mehera J. Irani, of whom he said that as Radha was to Krishna, Mehera is to me. Meher Baba was never married and maintained the highest code of moral discipline.

The two groups above and below show Meher Baba at Meherabad in 1938 with his Eastern and Western disciples. The photograph above shows Baba flanked by his mother Shireen *(left)* and his spiritual mother Daulatmai *(right)*. The photograph below shows the Western women dressed up in Indian saris.

In the December of 1938 Baba left Meherabad accompanied by over 20 men and women disciples in a specially designed bus. Fifteen large towns were visited. This tour of India lasted five months until the May of 1939. During the tour, a number of men disciples would go ahead by train to look for accommodations and arrangements in all the towns visited. Baba planned a visit for those accompanying him to Mathura, where Krishna was born and to Brindaban, which was the scene of Krishna's childhood, where he had woven around the gopis and cowherds the magic of his love and playfulness with the melody of his flute. As Baba and his disciples approached the river at Brindaban, a young man was seen sitting on the wall, playing a flute; when he noticed

Baba he stopped and in a loud voice cried out: 'Here comes the Flute Player' (which is another name for Krishna). He did not ask for anything but just ran ahead of Baba and began to dance to the music of his own flute. The guide thought Baba was being bothered and tried to drive the man away with a stick. Baba said: "Let him be." The young man kept on following Baba, shouting loudly, happily, "Krishna is here! Krishna is here!" Then it was time to return to the bus. Baba and the man greeted each other for the last time — there was an unmistakable sign of recognition written on his face. On the way back his followers asked him who the young man really was. Baba told them that he had come for this man who was a spiritually mature soul.

On a visit to several places of pilgrimage in 1938-39, Baba stopped midway between Jabalpur and Benares at Katni and stayed in the room occupied earlier by Upasni Maharaj.

Meher Baba was very fond of animals. Here he is seen at Alwar in 1938 holding a lamb in his arms.

48

While Baba worked with the masts at Bangalore, he also proposed to establish an International Spiritual Centre. This Centre would be at Byramgula, some twenty-two miles from Bangalore. Baba wanted this Centre to accommodate two thousand people of all religions, with six departments: The Spiritual Academy with the aim of preparation for international harmony; The House of Advanced Souls, for practical mysticism; The Abode of the Saints, for those who would teach of the Reality of God; the Mast Department, for the God-intoxicated; The Department of Meditation, for those who wished to practise meditation, under guidance; The Resting Place for the Afflicted, for the care and alleviation of suffering of all kinds. The plans for the Centre were abandoned at the start of the Second World War.

(Left) Meher Baba with his family *(left to right):* Adi, Jr., Mani, Meher Baba, Shireen, Jal and Behram. Baba's brothers and sister dedicated their lives to Baba and helped with his external spiritual work. Baba, who loved and respected his mother intensely, is seen with her at Bangalore in 1939 *(Above)*.

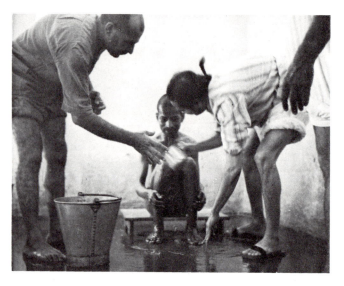

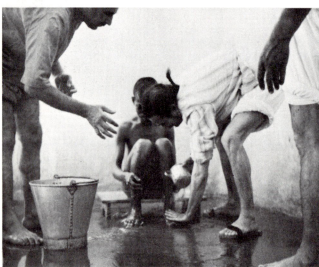

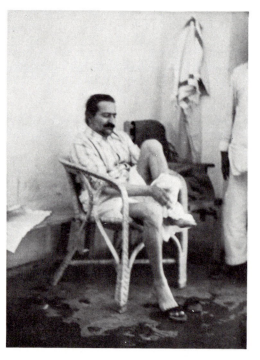

At the Bangalore Mast Ashram in 1939-40. Baba bathed and cleaned the masts and washed their latrines daily.

50

Baba had worked with the masts for a considerably long period. He dissolved the Bangalore mast ashram and returned to Meherabad in April 1940.[32] Here too he immediately resumed his work with the masts. For the first few days he would come to bathe them at 5:30 in the morning. But war had started and his own work took on the stress of the emergency. Now his work started at midnight. Apart from this work, the rest of the time he spent in seclusion.

[32] For most of Baba's Western lovers who stayed with him in Bangalore in 1939-40, the period was one of happiness, constant activity and close proximity with their Beloved. Dr. William Donkin records in his diary on February 19, 1940: "Baba was looking radiantly noble, with hair let down and really glistening. He was a fine sight to look at, his phenomenal strength of character and his sort of mysterious spiritual beauty and radiance very much visible as he sat on his couch. Baba's face in repose is such a fusion of spiritual bliss and serenity, yet such sadness, which gives dignity and grandeur to the face."

Meher Baba with disciples near Bangalore in 1940

Meher Baba in 1941

Meher Baba in 1941

51

Friday, October 17, 1941 was a significant day in spiritual history — Upasni Maharaj and Meher Baba met in a secluded hut at Dahigaon, a village in Ahmednagar District. They had met after nineteen years, and for those who witnessed this momentous meeting it was an auspicious day because it was Guru Dwadashi, the twelfth day of the second fortnight of the month of Asho, which, as the name signifies, is dedicated to the Guru, the Master. **33**

33 F. H. Dadachanji records: ''Shri Upasni Maharaj during the last few years used to say that he earnestly wanted to see Meher Baba. On hearing such oft-repeated requests, Meher Baba told Gulmai that he would see Maharaj alone and only once.'' It was their last meeting on the evening of October 17. On Christmas eve, December 24, 1941, at 3:30 a.m., Maharaj, who was in his seventy-first year, passed on. During the sahavas (love-gathering) of 1954, Meher Baba told his lovers, "Only Maharaj and Babajan directly played the main roles. Babajan, in less than a millionth of a second, made me realize that I am God; and in the period of seven years Upasni Maharaj gave me the Divine Knowledge that I am the Avatar. Before Maharaj dropped his body, we physically met in a secluded place. And before I drop my body, I had to meet him, so I went to Sakori and bowed down to his shrine and told him, ''You know I am the Ancient One, Maharaj was perfection personified.''

Then in 1941, the mast ashram was closed down suddenly and completely. The War had entered the third year. Japan was driving her forces into India's eastern border. Baba issued a message on the 'Spiritual Significance of the War' in March 1942. He said: "War-effort will be justified or stand condemned not by the results which it produces, but by the ends by which it is inspired. The world has to face this war and go through its ordeal of fire, even at the cost of irreparable damage and irredeemable suffering; it is a necessary evil....

"Humanity has to emerge out of this dreadful war with spiritual integrity, with hearts free from the poison of malice or revenge, with minds disburdened of the blows given or received, with souls unscathed by suffering and filled with the spirit of unconditional surrender to the Divine Will. In spite of its attendant evils, this war plays its part in my mission of helping humanity to fulfil the divine plan on earth and to inherit the coming era of truth and love, of peace and universal brotherhood of spiritual understanding and unbounded creativity."

He gave the following explicit instructions to all his disciples:

1) They should be above party politics and should bear malice and ill-will towards none.

2) They should observe all the precautionary measures of war for civil population enforced by the Government of the day.

3) They should continue as usual to discharge their special duties and work for Baba's spiritual cause unless otherwise directed by him.

4) They should stick to their posts and appointments anywhere in India, under any circumstances, unless ordered by the Government.

5) They may undertake humanitarian and relief work of a non-sectarian character, without identifying themselves with any party or political organization, and strictly within the scope of time and leisure left over after the performance of spiritual duties enjoined by him.

6) They should extend spiritual solace and comfort to the people within the area of their contacts and influence, with a view to counteracting the panicky states of their minds.

7) Exceptional cases and circumstances, requiring readjustment of routine lives, could be communicated to him.

Meher Baba with Shireen not long
before her death. Baba was at
Mahableshwar in 1943 when Shireen
died. On receiving the news at night,
Baba at once went to Poona. Shireen
loved Baba intensely and stayed with
the women mandali for weeks at a
time. She died at the age of sixty-
five on February 25, 1943, coinciding
with her son Meher Baba's birthday.

In the October of 1943, Baba and a large group of disciples
visited Calcutta during the terrible famine of that year, when
millions died of hunger. [34] During this visit, Baba fed about a
thousand people, organized the distribution of about ten thousand
chappaties (baked bread) and distributed vests to two thousand
children.

To the feast, organized at the Puddopukkur Relief Centre, were
invited some middle class people who, because of their social
position, could not ask for charitable relief.

When all were seated in the school building where the feast
was being given, some of the orthodox Hindus were disconcerted
at being served by a non-Hindu, i.e. by Baba, whose identity
was kept secret. However, the social workers of Calcutta who had
helped organize the feast explained to the guests that these
people (Baba and his disciples) had come all the way from Bombay
to serve them, and that they should be grateful. Nearly all accepted
this generosity and were even struck by the fact that the
originator of the charity had himself come to serve them and
supervise the work. When the feast was over, Baba personally
gave each person clothes and money.

[34] On an earlier visit to Calcutta in
June 1940, Baba met Karim Baba,
a sixth plane jalali mast. The
mandali named him 'the tiger man',
for he had long nails and skeins of
steel wire round his throat. His hair
and beard were thick, black, dirty
and matted. Despite the filth, his
face shone and there was fire in
his eyes. The mast was taken to
Ranchi where Baba fed him several
times a day and sat alone with him.

Baba and the Masts

35 Extracts from Dr. William Donkin's diary:

28-2-1940: Baba started his fast last Friday, 23rd and has been on honey water and lemon juice ever since. He is staying in the Mast Ashram, all of us men seeing him daily. He feeds the masts daily, and will not rest although he is fasting. Today he seems very tired — he washed the masts as well as fed them, and massaged all over the fat old one who is on the 6th plane. This evening Baba has vague pains in shoulder, neck and stomach....

13-4-1940: Panjim (Goa) we got here on Thursday morning after some trouble with the Portuguese customs; Baba said the man was good and within his rights to see some luggage from the top of the bus. On reaching Old Goa at the Church Xavier, Baba sent Elizabeth (Patterson) into a restaurant by the roadside to inquire when the church was open. She came out with an old man with long hair and beard, an old solar hat and a very old suit. Then the same evening we went along to see St. Francis Xavier's tomb, and on leaving, out came this old man and started chatting about dramas he had written in Karachi. He spoke good English and talked to us, kept glancing quickly at Baba. He was here writing a book, he said, about the place. He was a Catholic.

Baba told Jal to ask him if he required any help. He said, ''No thanks.'' Afterwards, Baba told us we were all blind and didn't see at the time that he was Baba's agent. He was a very advanced, conscious agent and that all his talk about dramas had inner meaning and that he was talking to Baba all the time. Baba told us he would leave us the next day. On the following day Elizabeth met him again and he told her that he was leaving at once; he felt he must go to a cold country, he didn't know if it was

The romance of Meher Baba and the masts forms the basis of a magnificent book 'The Wayfarers' by Dr. William Donkin. 35 The material is fascinating and here I mention some of the glimpses. Mian Saheb was a very spiritually advanced mast who lived in Ajanta. It was believed that he was over one hundred years old and deeply respected in Ajanta. People gave him whatever he asked for and a local businessman had given him a garden. In November 1944 Baba drove over to Ajanta from Aurangabad. When the party arrived one of the group proposed a meeting with Baba, and Mian Saheb suggested the use of a room on the upper floor of a certain house. Baba and the mast climbed to the room on the upper floor and were there for some time. Mian Saheb invited Baba to sit upon a sofa and then sat next to Baba, embraced him very lovingly. Then he started weeping loudly. Those waiting below could hear the mast weeping. The mast's tear-slurred voice recited a Persian couplet, ''Khud be Khud azad budi, khud gireftar amadi''; which means in free translation, ''You became free, and then allowed yourself to be bound.'' The allusion was clear; he was talking of Baba's Infinite state, and how he became bound of his own will to help humanity.

A greater part of 1945 was spent in Hyderabad where Baba contacted a large number of masts. One such important contact made in the summer of that year is described as follows: ''The spiritual chargeman of Hyderabad is Saiyed Moeinuddin (also called Majzoob Mian), a majzoob-like mast of the sixth plane, and typically jalali (fiery). He is a lame, elderly man who lives in a woodstall at the Fateh Gate in Hyderabad. He sweeps the road with his hands, is very fond of barfi (a sweetmeat), and he smokes exclusively an atrocious brand of cheap, local cigarettes. Because of his jalali nature, he was never easy to contact, and at the first attempt to meet him, Baba and his group were repulsed with epithets.'' Later after much resistance Baba contacted him successfully nearly four times in different situations.

Baba contacted a large number of spiritually advanced masts in 1946 who acknowledged Baba's spiritual greatness, despite the fact that he contacted them incognito and they had no tangible means of knowing who Baba was. Aghori Baba, a sixth plane mast of Simla when contacted in August, spoke, pointing to Baba and addressing those around him, ''You will see what will come to pass, and one day you will know who he (Baba) really is.'' When Baba contacted Azim Khan Baba on October 14, 1946, he said, "You are Allah; you have brought forth the creation, and once in a thousand years you come down to see the play of what you have created."

The same month, Pir Fazl Shah, an adept pilgrim of Kotah told Baba, "No one, until you came, has touched my heart with the arrow of Divine Love. You have the power to destroy and flood the whole world. No one fully knows the limits of your greatness; you are the spiritual authority of the time, and if I were to die I would take another body to be close to you."

Once again in the August of 1947 Baba toured Hyderabad extensively, contacted a large number of important masts, returned by the end of the same month and went into seclusion in a cabin built on the summit of a small hill called Tembi, near Meherazad.

his beard, but he felt all on fire. (Those readers who know a little about initiations, will recognize that this feeling which he had denoted Baba's spiritual working for him.) He had intended to stay a long time, but now he must go, he said — just as Baba had told us.

Baba at Mahableshwar in April, 1946. He continued with his mast work here and bathed and cleaned a number of God-mad men. Baba would sit alone with them for long periods.

Seclusion Hill (also known as Tembi Hill)

36 On the evening of December 5, 1947, Baba went into seclusion on Tembi Hill, behind Meherazad. Two small huts of cement asbestos sheeting had been erected — one on the summit of the hill and the other on a lower shoulder of the hill. Ali Shah, a mast was brought to Baba on this hill and he stayed in the lower of the two huts. Each morning, beginning on December 6 to December 17, Baba sat with him in the lower hut from 6 a.m. to 9 a.m.

36 For Baba the year 1948 was another year of hectic activities with masts and a significant visit to Allahabad to the Kumbh Mela where Baba contacted and touched the feet of 4,000 sadhus, among whom, he said, there were but seven advanced souls. On New Year's day in 1949 Baba sent the following circular from Meherazad: "All men and women who believe in me should observe silence for one full month in July 1949. All disciples and devotees to be more engrossed in God than in Maya by being less selfish and more sacrificing. The year 1949 marks an artificial end to an artificial beginning and the real beginning to the real end. Although I am in everyone and in everything and my work is for the spiritual awakening of all mankind, I am always aloof from politics of any kind. My disciples and devotees should continue as before to abstain from taking part in political activities and discussions."

From June 22 to July 31, 1949, Baba entered into forty days of seclusion at Meherazad. There had been many periods of seclusion in Baba's life, some for long periods, but this was known as the "Great Seclusion" because of the tremendous work Baba accomplished.

Around April 10, 1948 when this photograph was taken, Baba, along with five men and nine coolies, toured Uttarkashi. They were tired out and their feet blistered, but nevertheless, Baba continued to contact not only masts but sadhus, saints, initiates and adepts — altogether about fifty-nine men.

The New Life

On October 10, 1949, Meher Baba issued a very important circular: "Baba ends his Old Life of cherished hopes and multifarious activities, and with a few companions begins his New Life of complete renunciation and absolute helplessness from 16th October 1949...." This New Life of Baba and his companions was governed by severe conditions and oaths, wherein, amongst other things, one chief condition was that money was not to be touched. The main activity associated with this life was that of begging by Baba and his companions. While begging, Baba wore a green turban, walked bare-headed and bare-footed, wore a white kafni (robe) with an ochre-coloured satchel and carried a brass pot in the right hand.

On November 24, 1949, before going out for begging in Benares, Baba asked his companions to come before him after washing their feet. He then touched the feet of his companions with his forehead. Baba then had the following prayer read out: "I ask the most merciful God to forgive me and my companions for any shortcomings and any conscious and unconscious mistakes done singly or wholly or towards each other, or personally or impersonally, relating to the conditions or otherwise, as also for any lusty, angry, greedy or 'Old Life' thoughts or desires....

"I forgive you, my companions and ask you all to forgive me. I ask God to forgive us all not merely by way of ceremony but as a whole-hearted pardon."

Earlier in August Baba had held an important meeting at Meherabad where he had discussed the questions of movable and immovable properties, and provision for dependent families and those who might not be able to remain with him in the future. "I have no cash," he said, "except an amount which is kept aside for a certain work. Everything I possess including ashram buildings, fields and houses, etc., both here (Ahmednagar, Arangaon and Pimpalgaon) and elsewhere and all furniture, cars, power-plants, cattle, chattels and in fact everything that belongs to me, is to be disposed of. Nothing is to remain as my property and in my name except the Meherabad Hill premises on which the tomb for my bodily remains has already been built and all should always remember that when I leave my body it has always to be buried there."

Baba invited the mandali to give their whole-hearted cooperation in the task ahead of him and he warned them again and again to

Baba and Adi K. Irani go out for 'bhiksha' at Benares during the New Life phase in 1949. Baba and his companions wore long white robes (kafnis) with a 'jholi' (a cloth sack usually of ochre colour) slung across their shoulders. The 'jholi' had three compartments — one for grain, one for flour and one for cooked food, whatever was given. On Baba's 'jholi' Mehera had stitched the words 'Premse bhiksha deejeeai' meaning 'with love give alms.' Baba's instructions were that they should ask at one house only; if refused, they should go to the next.

discard all fads, fancies, notions and vagueness, particularly in respect of spiritual leanings and beliefs. They were asked to look upon the prospect of going with Baba without expectation of any reward whatsoever, spiritual and material.

The twenty companions of Baba in the New Life included four women: Mehera J. Irani, Mani S. Irani, Mehru R. Irani and Dr. Goher R. Irani and sixteen men: Adi K. Irani, Dr. William Donkin, Gustadji N. Hansotia, Dr. Nilkanth Godse (Nilu), Dr. A. Ghani Munsiff, A. R. Irani (Pendu), Sadashiv Shelke (Patel), Vishnu N. Deorukhkar, Murli R. Kale, Anna Jakkal, Babadas Dharmare, Dr. Dr. Daulat Singh, A. S. Baria (Kaka), R. B. Baiduliyan (Aga Baidul), Ali Akbar (Aloba) and Eruch B. Jessawala. **37**

During the period of the New Life Baba travelled extensively, staying for some time at Dehra Dun where he put before his companions several alternative plans for carrying on the New Life. Here Baba swept his own hut, cleaned his own utensils and washed his own clothes. The entire party ate only one meal a day. In March 1950, Baba with seven companions went to Rishikesh where he contacted sadhus, saints and mahatmas in their huts and caves. From Rishikesh he moved on to Motichur, Hardwar, Saatsarovar and other places. Baba explained that these contacts were very different from what he had made in the Old Life and that it was very important for his work. The task was very exacting for both Baba and his mandali. By the middle of the month, the total number of men contacted had reached 1,325 and by April 7 of the same year, when the work ended, the number had risen to 4,510.

37 Naosherwan Anzar: According to you, what is the importance of the New Life?

Eruch Jessawala: When we set out for the New Life, my only aim was to follow Baba, wherever he went. I never thought of any end result. In fact, none of us thought of any material or spiritual benefits which would accrue from following Baba into this new phase. We, as his mandali, fulfilled his every wish and whim and obeyed him whole-heartedly and without any reservations.

THE GLOW, February 1973

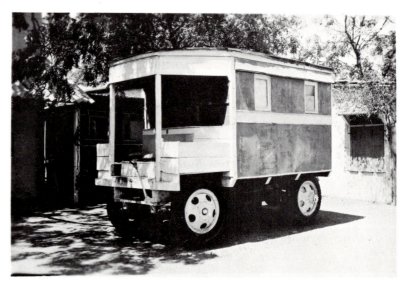

The New Life caravan was drawn by two bullocks. One of the bullocks drawing the caravan was Raja, an English bull, which Baba had fed milk from a feeding bottle when it was a calf in Meherabad.

Dehra Dun was the last destination for the bullock-drawn caravan which had transported Baba's women mandali over hundreds of miles. The bullocks were given away to a Baba lover and the caravan sent back to Ahmednagar.

During Baba's stay at Dehra Dun in 1950, he accepted 'bhiksha' from Keki R. Nalavala (the author's father) at Majri Mafi(now Meher Mafi), a village four miles from Dehra Dun.

The New Life was an extremely hard and important phase of Baba's life. He often talked on the subject. Baba said: "This New Life is endless, and even after my physical death it will be kept alive by those who live the life of complete renunciation of falsehood, lies, hatred, anger, greed and lust: and who, to accomplish all this, do no lustful actions, do no harm to anyone, do no backbiting, do not seek material possessions or power, who accept no homage, neither covet honour nor shun disgrace, and fear no one and nothing; by those who rely wholly and solely on God, and who love God purely for the sake of loving; and who believe in the lovers of God and in the reality of Manifestation, and yet do not expect any spiritual or material reward; who do not let go the hand of Truth, and who, without being upset by calamities, bravely and whole-heartedly face all hardships with one hundred per cent cheerfulness, and give no importance to caste, creed, and religious ceremonies.

"This New Life will live by itself eternally, even if there is no one to live it."

Meher Baba and his women mandali.

Baba touching the feet of a scavenger.
He made no class distinction and
said that this act alleviated the
sufferings of the poor.

On October 16, 1950, Baba invited
two hundred lovers to Mahableshwar,
where he gave a 'sermon' which
concluded: 'Let us love God as the
soul of our souls, for in the height of
this love lies this knowledge.'

Masts. Sadhus. Saints. The Poor. Baba's work went on with
them, through them. The time was 1950, October. He had travelled
far — Andhra Pradesh, Bihar, West Bengal, Orissa, Madras, Bombay
and far away Nepal. His name was not known to anyone on these
tours; he was simply referred to as 'Elder Brother.' Then from
February 13, 1951, Baba went into seclusion for about one hundred
days in Mahabaleshwar. In August, he declared the start of the
four months' work of the Mano-nash period — the period of
annihilation of the mind. Baba had explained the significance
thus: "Mano-nash results in this glorious state in which plurality
goes and Unity comes, ignorance goes and Knowledge comes,
binding goes and Freedom comes. We are all in this shoreless
Ocean of Infinite Knowledge, and yet are ignorant of it until the
mind — which is the source of ignorance — vanishes forever; for
ignorance ceases to exist when the mind ceases to exist.

"Unless and until ignorance is removed and Knowledge is
gained — the Knowledge whereby the Divine Life is experienced
and lived — everything pertaining to the Spiritual is paradoxical.

"God, whom we do not see, we say is real; and the world,
which we do see, we say is false. In experience, what exists for
us does not really exist; and what does not exist for us, really
exists.

"We must lose ourselves in order to find ourselves; thus loss
itself is gain.

"We must die to self to live in God: thus death means Life.

"We must become completely void inside to be completely
possessed by God: thus complete emptiness means absolute
Fullness.

"We must become naked of selfhood by possessing nothing, so
as to be absorbed in the infinity of God: thus nothing means
Everything."

The New Life was the voluntary suspension of the state of
Perfect Master to become a common man and a Perfect Seeker.
This had now been accomplished, and as Baba himself said, he
was free.

During the first twenty-four months of his New Life, Baba
passed through extremes of labour, mental strain and irregularities
of living. The last four months of the Mano-nash period he suffered
still more. Different types of work undertaken and performed by
him at different times during the New Life were successful; but
the tremendous strain on his physique wore him out completely.

In September 1954, Baba called a meeting of his Eastern and Western lovers. Here Baba is seen conversing with his lovers through the means of an alphabet board, while Eruch Jessawala is interpreting his indications on the board. On this very day Baba had his 'Final Declaration' read out.

63

The Free Life

Until July 10, 1952, Baba continued with his 'Complicated Free Life,' in which "bindings would dominate freedom." Then from November 15 started the 'Fiery Free Life,' in which "freedom and bindings would by the grace of God be merged into the Divine Life!" During this second period Baba made several comments on this phase of life: "I have no connection with politics. All religions are equal to me. And all castes and creeds are dear to me. But though I appreciate all 'isms,' religions and political parties, the absolute truth, while equally including them, transcends all of them and leaves no room for separative divisions, which are all equally false. The unity of all life is integral and indivisible. It remains unassailable and inviolable, in spite of all conceivable ideological differences."

He declared: "The result of this Fiery Free Life will make the world understand that Meher Baba and every one is one with God."

Even though Baba maintained absolute silence, every gesture and sign was correctly interpreted. The alphabet board, which Baba later discarded, was only a means for the interpreter to understand 'his language.'

Baba playing cricket near Satara. In his boyhood days he enjoyed playing cricket and was a fine batsman. He played marbles, seven tiles and charades and said that he did spiritual work through the concentrated energies of the players.

In April of 1952 Baba with five men and six women members of his mandali visited America. He stayed at the Meher Spiritual Center at Myrtle Beach, South Carolina, where two of his American disciples, Elizabeth Patterson and Norina Matchabelli had established a retreat for him. The retreat covered a sprawling 500 acres. At the Center a big house was erected for him and his men companions and a guest house for the women. A large cypress wood barn was used for meetings and interviews. At the various sahavas gatherings which Baba gave, people came from many parts of the country and Baba met them individually or in small groups. He told Elizabeth Patterson that the Center was to be devoted to the following purposes: a spiritual academy; a house of advanced souls; an abode of the saints; a 'mad' institute; as solitary quarters for meditation; and a resting place for the afflicted. Baba also said that this Center was his home in the West and one day it would become a place of pilgrimage.

On May 24 while proceeding to Meher Mount, Ojai, California, Baba and the women mandali were involved in a serious accident with an oncoming car. Baba was thrown out of the vehicle, his head bleeding and his left arm and left leg fractured. While the women members in the car were badly hurt, some with fractured arms, wrists and broken ribs, Baba was the only one to have lost blood. He had previously prophesied that he would shed blood on American soil, and here he was bleeding profusely.[39] On June 13, Baba issued a statement: ''The personal disaster for some years foretold by me has at last happened while crossing the American continent causing me through facial injuries, a broken leg and arm, much mental and physical suffering. It was necessary that it should happen in America. God willed it so....''

39
''When I finally got round to attending to Baba I was surprised to see an individual who was injured as badly as he was, still smiling. I was also astounded to find that he did not speak a word or make any sound denoting discomfort. I assumed that he could not, but was informed soon by Dr. Irani that he did not speak because of a willful act. I knew that we were going to have to give him a general anesthetic (pentothal) to set his fractures and suspected that he would say something at that time, but he didn't. The most attractive quality of his personality that first day was the way he would look at me with those big brown eyes as if he were reading my mind.''

Dr. Burleson
Surgeon of the Prague Clinic
Prague, Oklahoma, U.S.A.

Sufism Reoriented

"I am equally approachable to one and all big and small,
To saints who rise and to sinners who fall,
Through all the various paths that give the divine call.
I am approachable alike to saint whom I adore
And to sinner whom I am for,
And equally through Sufism, Vedantism, Christianity,
Or Zoroastrianism and Buddhism and other isms
Of any kind and also directly through no medium of isms at all."

On July 20, 1952, Baba had the above message pinned on the bulletin board during his stay in New York. Baba addressed the Sufi group: "If you take Baba to be perfect and one with God, Baba is then the Ocean — and these different paths, Sufism, Vedantism, Zoroastrianism, Buddhism, Jainism and Christianity are as Rivers to the Ocean. But now the time has arrived when these Rivers have more or less become dry. Those who follow these different paths do it only in form. More importance is given to ceremonies and practices, but the real purpose is lost sight of."

Baba stated that these Rivers had gone dry and so the Ocean itself had to go out and flood the Rivers. "So it is now time for me to re-orient these different isms which end in One God. I intend to make one unique charter regarding this re-oriented Sufism and send it to Ivy Duce from India in November, with my signature, and entrust the American Sufism work to her. This Charter will have an entirely new aspect but not lose its originality. Now when I send the Charter and the Constitution, and the instructions, it will be applicable to the whole Sufi world — and will, by God's grace — be lasting in its effect and influence."

Sufism as reoriented by Meher Baba is based on love and longing for God and the eventual union with God in actual experience. The Charter states that it is the duty of every member: (a) to become conversant with the principles of Sufism by reading and studying the literature of Sufi saints, poets and authors such as Hafiz, Jalaluddin, Shams, Inayat Khan, Ibn Arabi, Shibli, Hujwiri and others; (b) to necessarily read and study vigorously the Discourses by Meher Baba and the book by Meher Baba called "God Speaks" which depicts the ten states of God and other important truths, and which is his last and final book on this subject; (c) to necessarily repeat verbally daily one name of God for half an hour at any time of the day or night; this is to be done consecutively if possible, but may be accomplished in smaller portions if necessary; (d) to meditate on the Master daily for fifteen minutes in any secluded spot.

In July, Baba left Myrtle Beach for New York where he gave personal interviews and discourses. He returned to India in November for the darshan that was to last thirty-five days. Despite the pain and suffering which the accident had caused him, Baba sought different people and visited many towns and remote villages. He traversed forests, hills, crossed rivers and streams, often going to places where no vehicle had ever been before. Wherever Baba went, crowds of people received him. They came on foot, horses, bullock-carts and camels. In fact some said they had been waiting for several years to see him.

Baba washed the feet of several poor people wherever he went and he bowed down to them and gave them money in gratitude, for he said that the poor were sharing the burden of the spiritual upliftment of humanity and were a great help in his work. He also gave mass darshans to the people who gathered at various places. To each man, woman and child, he gave some sweet or fruits as prasad. Baba's messages and statements were read to the people and translated into local languages. Thousands came to take his blessings and many more came from far off places just to get a glimpse of him. One man came from a distance of 27 miles rolling on the ground, without having taken any food till he had met Baba. Baba embraced him lovingly and gave him fruit with which he broke his fast. Meher Baba's charisma was overwhelming. His face cast a spell on the onlookers and exuded serenity and composure. His presence made everybody aware of his all-embracing love. Those who came to him for redress went away with hope and cheer. Although he did not speak in words, his eyes and fingers spoke all the time, with his interpreter uttering his thoughts. [40]

On February 16, 1953 Baba went to Dehra Dun and went into seclusion for the rest of the year. From August 13 to September 2, he was engaged in intense universal work during which he had the Master's Prayer, composed by him for his lovers, recited in his presence. It was at this time his Fiery Free Life had reached its culmination. On September 7, 1953, Baba made one of his most important announcements declaring in clear terms his role as the God-Man. (See Appendix for complete text.)

The world was going through times of stress. Political turmoils and tensions were rife. Baba's disciples gathered before their Master asking him to alleviate their sufferings and he told them,

[40] Baba, what is life?
BABA: Life is a mighty joke. He who knows this can hardly be understood by others. He who does not know it finds himself in a state of delusion. He may ponder over this problem day and night but will find himself incapable of knowing it. Why? Because people take life seriously, and God lightly; whereas we must take God seriously and life lightly. Then we know that we always were the same and will ever remain the same...the Originator of this Joke. This Knowledge is not achieved by reasoning, but it is the Knowledge of Experience.
Dehra Dun
March 23, 1953

"I know and understand your difficulties and problems, sufferings and expectations. Not only the individuals, but the whole world is in the **throes** of sufferings. When suffering comes, it comes according to the definitely established law of Karma. It must then be accepted with grace and fortitude. But it must be remembered that your actions are the cause of much of your sufferings. Through wise actions it can be minimized. What humanity needs is spiritual wisdom; and for this, it must inevitably turn to the Perfect Masters and Avatars."

Tour of South India

In January 1954, Baba visited Andhra Pradesh and later went to Madras where he gave darshan to nearly 150,000 people. The travelling went on. At Bezwada Baba sat with the people and told them that he wanted them to feel that he was one of them and that was why he was sitting with them on the ground. He said, "I am on the level of each one of you. Whether poor, rich, small, big, I am like each of you, but I am approachable only to those who love me." On his birthday, which was celebrated at Tadepalligudam, he gave a message: "I am never born. I never die. Yet every moment I take birth and undergo death. The countless illusory births and deaths are necessary landmarks in the progression of man's consciousness to Truth — a prelude to the Real Death and Real Birth. The Real Death is when one dies to self; and the Real Birth is when, dying to self, one is born in God to live for ever His Eternal Life consciously." [41] At Rajamundry Baba addressed a large gathering of his followers and Baba-workers. The meeting was held on March 1 and it went on from 9:00 p.m. until 3:00 a.m. the following morning. Baba spoke to them about what he meant by doing real work for Baba. (See Appendix for complete text.)

The tour of South India ended at Kakinada on March 24 where he gave his last message: "It has been possible through Love for man to become God; and when God becomes man, it is due to His love for His beings. If people were to ask me, 'Have you seen God?' I would reply 'What else is there to see?' If they were to ask me, 'Are you God?' I would reply 'Who else could I be?' If they were to ask me, 'Are you Avatar?' I would reply 'Why else have I taken this human form?'"

[41] *Extract from Kishan Singh's diary: 21-2-1954:* After resting awhile Baba, on a specific invitation conveyed through his lovers, visited the Sai Baba Samaj at Guntur. There he sat on the ground, although a well-decorated chair was placed for him. At the request of the Samaj members, Baba touched Sai Baba's photograph as well as the foundation stone for a proposed temple. Baba then dictated: "I feel very happy on this occasion. This grand old man was and is a unique personality in the spiritual world; and he knows, and only a few like him who are the personification of Perfection know, that I am the Ancient One."

In Bezwada during his 1954 tour of Andhra, on February 21 at 4 p.m., Baba said, ''Whether poor, rich, small, big, I am like each of you; but I am approachable only to those who love me''

69

Baba distributing 'prasad'. It was a
love-gift consisting of a sweetmeat,
fruit, flowers, cereals or even cash
gifts to the poor. It formed a close
intimacy with the Master and had
tremendous spiritual significance.
During his tour of Andhra in 1954 he
gave 'darshan' to many thousands of
people and 'prasad' to an equal
number.

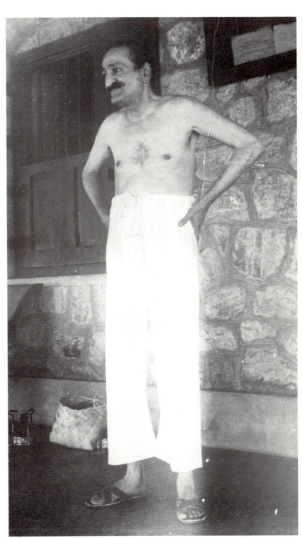

Whether he travelled in the East or the West he always mingled with his lovers, sat in their midst and declared: 'I am on the level of each one of you.'

Baba at Tadepalligudam (Andhra) on his birthday. On the occasion Baba said, ''Now I will give my 'prasad' (in this case bananas) of love, which you accept with love. No one should bow down to me or offer fruits and flowers. Only take with love, what I give with love.''

On October 7, 1954 Baba gave up the use of the alphabet board. On November 6, he visited Pandharpur at the invitation of Gadge Maharaj. Baba had told Maharaj that he would not give darshan to the masses, nor take food or sleep, but would make himself available to the pilgrims. Baba visited the leper colony there and washed and cleaned the lepers.

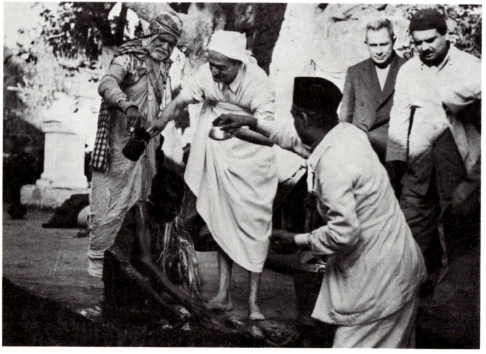

Baba playing on a pair of Indian cymbals in accompaniment to the bhajans sung.

Meher Baba invited men only from the East and the West for special meetings to be held on September 29 and 30, 1954, at Meherabad. Earlier, on September 12, Baba gave darshan to a great crowd of people in Ahmednagar. On this occasion he said, "Not as man to man, but as God to God, I bow down to you to save you the trouble of bowing down to me" and prostrated himself before the people. Baba sat with the crowd and told them, "To make you share all my feelings of being with you and one of you, I sit down beside you." [42] Baba gave two very significant messages during this darshan programme (see Appendix for complete text). This darshan was by far the most touching event as men, women and children filed past Baba in obeisance while he gave each of them a sweet delicacy. The crowd ranged from beggars in tattered clothes to well-dressed men and women. By the time it was over, nearly 100,000 people had had darshan.

[42] *Extract from Kishan Singh's diary: 30-9-1954: On entering Upper Mcherabad, Baba walked straight into the Tomb followed by those who were accompanying him. He asked all to sit down on the platform and at 09.10 hours said:*

"This was the place of my seclusion when I sat for one year continuously. In this place you will find a trench-like opening where I stayed day and night and confined myself in seclusion.

"The period spread over one year, 1927-28. I was not taking any solid food, only coffee. I had deputed a Harijan boy named Lahu to bring a full flask of coffee. Before sitting in seclusion here I had instructed the women mandali to prepare a flask full of coffee and send it to me to last for the day. But every day I received half a flask of coffee. After completion of the year long seclusion, I asked the ladies why they had been sending me only a half flask full. The women mandali assured me that they sent a full flask.

"I then called the little boy Lahu, embraced him and asked him to tell the truth. He confessed, 'Baba, while bringing the coffee daily, I felt hungry and drank half the flask of coffee every day.'

"In this way for one year I took that boy's 'prasad' of (partly drunk) coffee."

Baba visited Hyderabad on January 15, 1951 with four companions. He said his visit was to complete his work with masts and the poor.

74

The Love Gathering

The scheduled meeting with his Western lovers towards the end of September was another important event when Baba gave several discourses and answered many questions. One of the Western lovers remarked to Baba that the darshan programme must have been a great strain on his body. "Before I drop my body," Baba replied, "I shall go through violent attacks on the body. What has to happen will happen and I will gladly undergo all this for the sake of humanity. My only happiness lies in making people understand, not through the mind, but through experience, that God alone is the Beloved for whom we exist." [43] On yet another day, on his return from Sakori where he had taken his Western lovers, Baba was asked to speak on miracles. He said: "Many miracles have been attributed to me, but I do not perform miracles. When people think that miracles have been performed, their faith has done it. One miracle I will perform, and for that miracle the time is nigh. I have said that my miracle will be not to raise the dead but to make one dead to himself and live for God. I have repeatedly said that I will not give sight to the blind, but I will make them blind to the world in order to see God." At the same meeting Baba had his 'official declaration' read out, in which he outlined the purpose of his advent. Soon after at the request of his lovers, Baba gave a clarification and confirmation of the 'final declaration' (see Appendix for complete text).

[43] When Baba suffered, his lovers cried for him. Their hearts would burst to see him crucified thus. Suffering the agony of Baba's crucifixion, I wrote to him beseeching to let me share his suffering. Baba wrote back: "My physical body, which alone is visible to your physical eyes, appears all affected and afflicted. But it is all due to the tremendous pressure of the burden of Universal Suffering that I shoulder on my Universal Body that tells upon my physical body — with which you are conversant and which is the only medium for you to see me and feel me in the gross world. Soon after I break my silence, all the Universal Suffering will end."

— Naosherwan

Photos on facing page:

Baba called a meeting of his Eastern and
Western male lovers in 1954. On Tuesday,
September 14, he took his Western lovers
up Meherabad Hill, showed them round his
Tomb, his cabin and several other structures
at Lower Meherabad which were associated
with his work over the years.

Photos right and below:

On Monday, September 20, Baba visited
the Ashram founded by Upasni Maharaj in
Sakori along with a party of his lovers.
Godavri and her women companions
received Baba devotedly; Baba said,
"...Godavri is the Mother here and all
are her companions. She met Maharaj
when two and a half years old. He
put her on his lap and said, 'All this
belongs to you.' They all live a life
dedicated to my Master. I love her
most dearly." Baba paid homage to
Maharaj by kneeling down and kissing
the stone on which was engraved
Maharaj's will.

During this momentous meeting of 1954, Baba gave darshan, distributed prasad and gave discourses to his lovers.

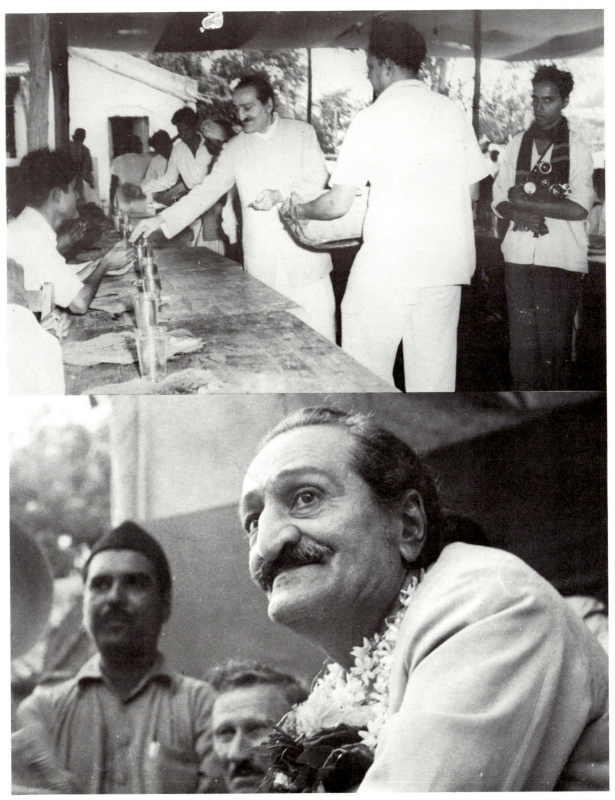

The Meherabad meeting brought the Beloved and his lovers in close intimacy. Baba looked to the welfare of the invitees and appeared radiant and cheerful, despite the strain of the various programmes.

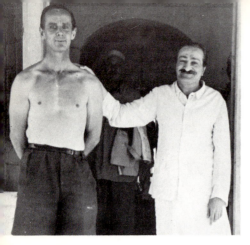

Meher Baba with Dr. Donkin
at Satara in 1955. **44**

⁴⁴ In December of 1946, in Mahableshwar, Meher Baba gave the task of writing the account of his work with masts and other advanced souls to Dr. William Donkin. What appeared in print was an incredibly detailed and expressive book called *The Wayfarers*. Before Dr. Donkin joined Baba's mandali, he was given time to complete his studies in medicine. William corresponded consistently with Baba and in reply to his longing to join Baba, he received beautiful letters from him. One such letter written by Baba and signed M. S. Irani from Meherabad, Ahmednagar, dated November 2, 1938, said:

Dear Donkin,

Well done! Now follow up with even better results. Do not relax your efforts by their first success. Big plans lie ahead here. These I will write about shortly and keep you informed of my movements. There is peace for the moment, but it will not be lasting. The bubble will burst shortly. The world as it is today can never make for peace, however hard one or two nations may desire it. Peace eventually there will be but only after such suffering as the world as yet has never seen. Then only will men turn their thoughts from money and selfishness to the things that are worthwhile. Externally war is a dreadful thing and unless it were absolutely necessary for the spiritual upheaval I would never allow a war to be. Now do not worry over anything. Be cheerful in deed, word, thought and in appearance, whatever you may be feeling inside.

Meanwhile, from October 7, 1954, Baba had given up the use of the alphabet board; now all communication was through finger signs and gestures. During November 1955, there was another sahavas programme, where he explained to the people several points of spiritual interest. He particularly talked of his early days and his activities (see Appendix for messages and discourses). On one of the sahavas days, a tall rugged man visited Baba. Baba pointed him out and said, "This is Satya Mang. Once he was a well-known and ruthless dacoit who terrorised this part of the country. He is now going straight, but is practically starving. He was attracted to me more than thirty years ago and soon became devoted enough to promise to give up robbery. That promise caused him a great struggle. After sometime, he could not help slipping back, and one night he set out to steal again. He succeeded with his plan, but just as he was about to take his loot, he saw me standing there before him. This reminded him of his promise and because of his love for me he was saved."

On the 3rd day of the Sahavas, a middle aged man rose from the group and asked permission to recite some Sanskrit verses. Baba gave him permission and he recited the verses so lovingly that he could not contain himself. He cried out 'Avatar Meher Baba ki jai,' broke into tears and asked forgiveness for his sins. Baba called the man to him, embraced him warmly, stroked his back, patted his cheeks and held him to his breast. "Don't be frightened," he said. "You need not tell me any more. If I am the Avatar then I know everything, and everything will be forgiven. If I am not the Avatar, what good will it do to you to tell me anything, and what use would it be to ask my forgiveness? I can forgive; I have come to forgive. Forgiveness is the highest thought for those who have forgiven. It is not a great thing to forgive. In fact, in reality, there is nothing to be forgiven, for there is really nothing like good and bad. You find them so and they are there in duality due to your own bindings in duality...." Among the remarks that Baba made later was, "After I drop this body, thousands upon thousands of people will come. So, age after age the same thing is repeated. No sooner do I drop the body, than people come to the tomb. When I go to give darshan, thousands of people flock around me. What is the use? If I am great, greatness does not consist in collecting crowds around me. What I want is a little love from you."

(Left) On October 27, 1955 Baba visited the Yeravada Central prison to make contact with an internee. The prison staff received him with courtesy and Baba continued to do his internal work. Several years earlier in 1931, Baba went to the Sing Sing Prison and his car was stopped outside the main entrance. Baba said to those with him, 'In this prison there is a man who is my agent; he does good work for me. I shall free him when I speak.'

In July and August of 1956, Baba toured the West, meeting with His lovers in Europe, the United States and Australia. During this time, he held six days of Sahavas for about one hundred devotees at Meher Spiritual Center in Myrtle Beach. A few weeks before he left India for his trip to the West, Baba issued the following message:

   "As declared in the past, I am free from promises and I am not bound by time and space. Though all happenings are in the realm of illusion, a great so-called tragedy is facing me and my lovers. My long-expected humiliation is near at hand. This may happen tomorrow or any day of this year, or it may happen next year.

   "The love, courage and faith of my lovers will be put to a severe test, not by me, but by Divine Law. Those who hold fast to me at the zenith of this crisis will transcend illusion and abide in Reality.

   "I want all my lovers to know that the contents of this circular, however despairing, should not affect their enthusiasm and the efforts of their preparations for my coming, because my humiliation and 'tragedy,' though necessary, are but passing phases which are bound to have a glorious end as is destined."

Meher Baba outside the author's home at Dehra Dun, 36 Lytton Road. 36 Lytton Road had become during the New Life Baba's link with the outside world. All correspondence came to this address and Baba visited the house several times.

During Baba's stay in New York in 1956, the American lovers gave Baba a dinner and reception at the Longchamps Restaurant. About 150 guests attended the reception, and it was filmed by movie cameras and for TV.

Baba in Lagoon Cabin at Myrtle Beach in 1956. He was given a loving reception by Elizabeth Patterson, Kitty Davy and the large number of lovers gathered at the Center.

Baba admiring the beauty of the vast expanse of the Myrtle Beach Center. The Center is spread over an area of 500 acres.

Disaster

Like Jesus. Like Buddha. Like Mohammed. When the Avatar comes to the earth, to live among men, he too must suffer, he too must bleed. On December 2, 1956, Baba had gone to Poona for a day. He was accompanied by Eruch, Pendu, Vishnu and Nilu, his mandali members. At around 4:45 p.m. of the same day, while returning to Satara, Baba and his party were involved in a severe accident which occurred about twelve miles outside Satara. The car was running normally and at moderate speed, when it seemed suddenly and inexplicably to go completely out of control and dashed against a stone culvert, landing eventually in a ditch on the other side of it. Baba and his men were badly injured and were immediately hospitalised, except Nilu who had died without regaining consciousness. Dr. William Donkin, who attended to Baba, wrote in a report: "Minor abrasions and subcutaneous contusions on the forehead, nose and cheeks; a tear of the upper and lower surface of the tongue, sutured a few hours after the accident; and the upper rim of the acetabulum has been fractured, the broken chip of bone being slightly displaced. Surgical attention is now concentrated on the treatment of the hip injury." Someone had asked Baba why, if he was the Avatar, was he the victim of so severe an accident and as to why he could not avert it. Baba replied, "What the Divine Will has decreed must and will happen, and if I am the Divine Personification you believe me to be then the last thing I would do is to avert or avoid it." He had explained this earlier: "People suffer for their Karma. A few suffer for others. Perfect Masters suffer for the universe." On the persistent query of Baba-lovers the world over enquiring of Baba's health, he said, "It is as if the mental sufferings of the universe want to crush me. But the Infinite Bliss I experience and the love I have for all sustains me; and the love of all my lovers supports me in the burden I carry...."

The Avatar will have his crucifixion. But his work must go on. That is the Divine Will. On February 12th and 15th, 1957, Baba touched the feet of 800 poor people at Meherazad and gave each of of them prasad of sweets and clothes. Soon afterwards, he visited Sakori and Poona where he gave darshan to thousands of people who had assembled there. The strain was immense, often painful and at times he had to move on crutches and at times had to be carried in a chair.

Meher Baba at Bindra House, Poona in 1957 after the accident near Satara

Baba in the wheel-chair at Meherazad in March 1957

Despite the hindrance of his leg in a plaster cast as a result of the accident, Baba gave darshan to hundreds of his lovers in the East and West.

In the meantime, in September 1956, Meher Baba's book 'God Speaks' was released in America. It outlined the theme of creation and its purpose. As to what it meant to the readers, the words of Dr. W. Y. Evans-Wentz stand out: "No other Teacher in our own time or in any known past time has so minutely analysed consciousness as Meher Baba has in 'God Speaks'....(This) enlightening treatise adds much to the sum total of learning and contributes incalculably to the enrichment of mankind...."

Meher Baba dedicated *GOD SPEAKS* 'to the Universe — the illusion that sustains Reality.'

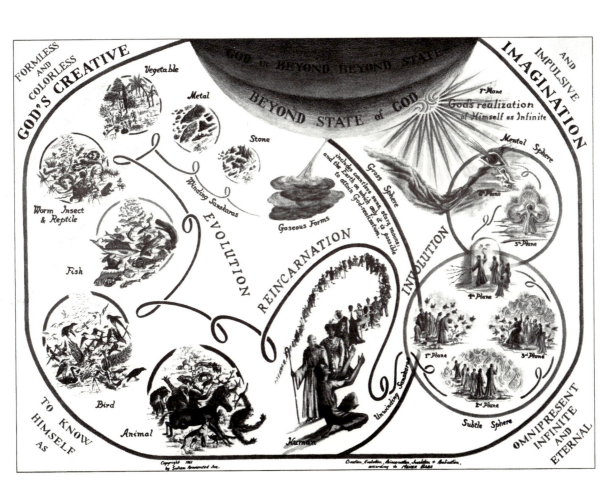

This chart, painted by Rano Gayley under the supervision of Meher Baba, is a pictorial version of the book *GOD SPEAKS*. It can be found in the second edition of *GOD SPEAKS*, published in 1973 by Sufism Reoriented, Inc.

On September 8, 1957, Baba distributed sweets to 32 men who were present at Meherazad. "Let me sweeten your mouths before I make you swallow some bitter pills." Baba said, "I am no saint. Because I am Beyond, I am therefore beyond all saints. The world, once it knows who I am, will understand then what I want you to understand now — that from the beginningless beginning, I am the Ancient One, immutable and eternal. You may whole-heartedly believe me to be the Avatar; but belief, however deep, does not amount to absolute conviction...."

Here D. interjected, "There is no question of conviction for those of us who have accepted you once and for all — because our acceptance is absolute." Baba continued, "It is all for the best if that acceptance remains unshaken under all circumstances. The world in general accepts the existence of God, without caring overmuch about the reasons for doing so. It is a fact, also, that there are a few in the world who do see God as He is to be seen, and fewer still who know God as He really is to be known." Baba warned his disciples of a 'dark cloud' hovering over the world and asked them to hold on fast to his daaman.

In February 1958, Baba held a sahavas for his Eastern lovers and in May went to Myrtle Beach again to be with his Western lovers. Before leaving for the West, he had given a message: "This sahavas will be unique in the sense that you will witness and share my present universal suffering by being near me as my fortunate companions — being with the Ancient One, who will be completely on the human level with you. It will be helpful to all participating in the sahavas to know of the hint I have given to those living with me — reminding them of my 'declaration' wherein I stated that my glorification will follow my humiliation, pointing out that this period of my sahavas will fall within the orbit of my universal suffering and helplessness.... I may give you more, much more, than you expect — or maybe nothing, and that nothing may prove to be everything. So I say, come with open hearts to receive much or nothing from your Divine Beloved. Come prepared to receive not so much of my words but of my Silence." **45** All who came for the sahavas stayed with Baba all the time; their allegiance to him was total, their obedience explicit. It was a very special sahavas packed with discourses and messages, explanations and dialogues. (see Appendix for selected messages). In early June, Baba visited Australia and returned to India after a short stay there.

45 Will you comment on what you mean by 'to come to me'? BABA: To come to me means liberation, experiencing me as I am. No more bondage of births and deaths. But it does not mean the state of a Perfect Master, or Perfection. That is only to be attained in the gross body. So if you are not blessed with this state of perfection, at least you can have liberation. If you just take my name, just at the moment of dropping your body, you will come to me. Yes, anyone. It's easy to take my name at the very moment of leaving the body. Then you individually experience bliss, infinite bliss. After liberation you continue to experience infinite bliss eternally. Why? Because it belongs to you eternally. You experience what belongs to you eternally. Even spiritual ecstasy cannot be compared with Divine Bliss. Remember this.

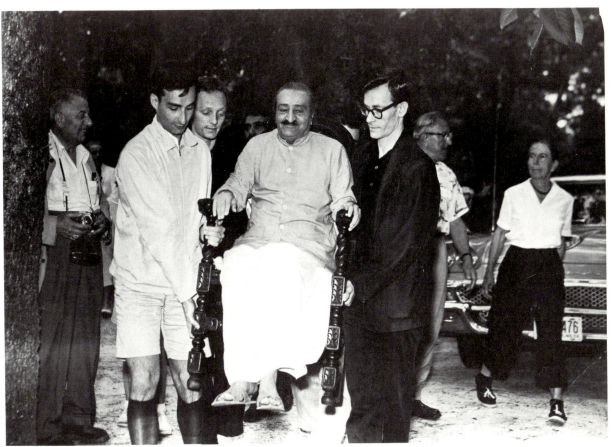

On Sunday, December 2, 1956, on the return journey to Satara from Poona, Baba's car crashed against a low stone culvert at the side of the road, turned over and landed in the gully. Baba sustained serious injuries: his head and face were badly hurt, his tongue torn, the right hip damaged (the upper rim of the acetabulum being fractured and the broken chip of bone slightly displaced). Despite the injuries Baba went in May 1958 to Myrtle Beach. He was often carried from place to place in a chair where he gave darshan, discourses and explanations to his lovers.

Universal Message

Among the many discourses and messages that Baba has given from time to time, the Universal Message is considered most important for its clarity and profundity:

I have come not to teach but to awaken. Understand therefore that I lay down no precepts.

Throughout eternity I have laid down principles and precepts, but mankind has ignored them. Man's inability to live God's words makes the Avatar's teaching a mockery. Instead of practising the compassion he taught, man has waged crusades in his name. Instead of living the humility, purity and truth of his words, man has given way to hatred, greed and violence.

Because man has been deaf to the principles and precepts laid down by God in the past, in this present avataric form I observe Silence. You have asked for and been given enough words — it is now time to live them. To get nearer and nearer to God you have to get further and further away from 'I,' 'Me,' and 'Mine.' You have not to renounce anything but your own self. It is as simple as that, though found to be almost impossible. It is possible for you to renounce your limited self by my Grace. I have come to release that Grace.

I repeat, I lay down no precepts. When I release the tide of Truth which I have come to give, men's daily lives will be the living precept. The words I have not spoken will come to life in them.

I veil myself from man by his own curtain of ignorance, and manifest my Glory to a few. My present avataric Form is the last Incarnation of this cycle of time, hence my Manifestation will be the greatest. When I break my Silence, the impact of my Love will be universal and all life in creation will know, feel and receive of it. It will help every individual to break himself free from his bondage in his own way. I am the Divine Beloved who loves you more than you can ever love yourself. The breaking of my Silence will help you to help yourself in knowing your real Self.

All this world confusion and chaos was inevitable and no one is to blame. What had to happen has happened; and what has to happen will happen. There was and is no way out except through my coming in your midst. I had to come, and I have come. I am the Ancient One.

In February 1959, Vilayat Khan, the son of Pir-o-Murshid
Inayat Khan, came to see Baba at Meherabad with a desire to sit
in meditation near a shrine in Ajmere and expressed his desire to
meditate on Baba in Baba's physical presence. Baba told him:
"Don't run away from the world: renounce your own lower self.
Silently cry out within your own self, 'Beloved One, reveal
yourself to me as my own real infinite self.' It is you who are
obstructing yourself from finding your self, so try to lose your
lower self in continued remembrance of God, who is your real
self. Don't become Master of disciples till you have mastered
your own self." The very next month Baba visited Bombay where he
he gave darshan to hundreds of people. At the end of the month
he returned to Poona and one day, during this period, he remarked,
"When I retire at night I feel as though my body has been wrung
out.... My general health is getting worse, yet I am getting much
more active. But it is not for reasons of health I now stop giving
darshan. It is for my universal work, which weighs on me heavily,
of which you can have no idea. The time is come. The universe
is come out of me and has to come into me." But the love of his
lovers for the Beloved was insatiable. On June 5, 1960, Baba
emerged from his seclusion and gave darshan to over ten thousand
people who had come from many parts of India and a few days
later he received and bowed down to 160 poor people by placing
his forehead on their feet. Baba once again went into seclusion,
and on the thirty-sixth anniversary of his silence on July 10, he
asked all those who love and obey him to observe complete
silence for twenty-four hours.

Baba in seclusion at the Guruprasad
Bungalow in Poona in the middle of
March 1961. He was still seriously ill;
nevertheless, for a fortnight in May he
gave one hour each afternoon for people
to visit him.

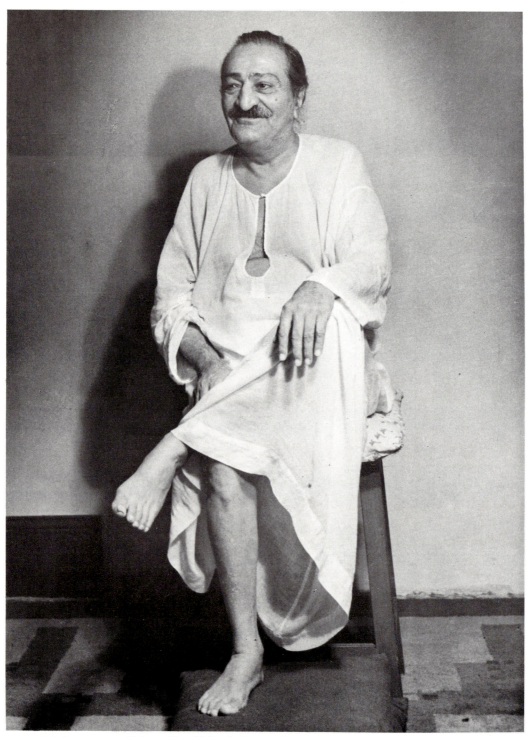

"I belong to no religion. My religion is Love. Every heart is my temple. Although it is in Love that you have built this house of stone, I am only in it when your heart brings me here. Always remember that ceremonies cover me, but pure love reveals me."

Meher Baba

Darshan

In November 1962 there was another darshan of his Eastern and Western followers in Poona. It was a unique event; for the first time in the history of mankind East and West met in oneness at the feet of the God-Man. Among those who had come from the West were doctors, lawyers, architects, professors and businessmen, students, teachers, farmers, ballet dancers, actors, as well as wives and mothers and some children. The Easterners were of all castes, classes and religions and came from India, Iran, Pakistan and the Middle East. Baba addressed this large gathering as 'My dear children' and said that 'All religions of the world proclaim that there is but one God, the Father of all in creation. I am that Father.'

At the unprecendented East-West gathering of 1962, Baba gave his blessings to thousands of his lovers and permitted special interviews to a group of Westerners who had travelled hundreds of miles to be with their Beloved.

Meher Baba in 1962. His hand gesture of making a circle with his thumb and index finger signified beauty and perfection.

One morning in 1963, a visitor from the Theosophical Society came to see Baba for the first time and asked him for a message. Baba said, "My message is love God to such an extent that you become God. That love is a gift from God. One of the means by which it can also be won is selfless service — but the selfless service should be so sublime that you should not even have a thought that you are serving!" And on yet another occasion Baba said, "God is not to be found in the skies or in the caves of the Himalayas. God is in the heart of each one. Once your heart is clean, God will shine out in it. But it is not easy to clean one's heart. It is like diving deep into a sea of fire! To love me is to lose yourself. Hence, where you are, God is not; and where God is, you are not. It is easy to become good but very difficult to become God." With tongue in cheek, one of the mandali remarked that it should be easy to become God after becoming 'good' — one just had to knock off an 'o.' Baba replied, "It is no joke to do that — even if one were to die in the attempt to knock off that 'o,' one would not succeed!"

Towards the end of the year, when news came of the assassination of the U. S. President, John F. Kennedy, Baba said of him: "He was a great man, good and sincere. Dying as he did has not only made him immortal in mankind's memory and history, but it has given him a great push forward spiritually. However, although he was assassinated because it was ordained to be, it is not a good thing and it portends more suffering ahead for the world." In a message on his birthday, Baba said that the aim of life was to love God and the goal of life is to become one with God. The surest and quickest way to achieve this goal is to hold on to his daaman by loving him more and more. He added, "I have suffered much and will have to suffer much more till I break my silence."

False Gurus

Meher Baba's secretary, Adi K. Irani issued a circular to all group heads in India on April 10, 1964. The letter stated that a man in Delhi called Krishnaji was trying to contact Baba-lovers. "This man is of South India (Kerala) and was for a time with Baba in Satara. Often he had confessed to the mandali that Baba's love and compassion had retrieved him from a life of degredation, and that he had not known what love was before he met Baba. Being by nature an exhibitionist, Krishnaji wore a robe and kept his hair long, but Baba directed him to discard such sham and had him dress in ordinary clothes. Although he lived with the mandali for a while, he could not accommodate himself to the simple life lived by Baba's men. Shortly he found that his presence in his home town was imperative due to some unpleasant affair he had been involved in, and beloved Baba instructed him to return home for good.

"Later this Krishnaji came to Delhi and reverting to robe and long hair began to observe periodic silence and to pose as the 'Chargeman of Meher Baba.' Now he calls himself 'Baba', claims to be observing complete silence and is said to communicate with visitors by means of an alphabet board."

A significant instance, this, as it reveals how Baba tried to guide his lovers and followers to distinguish the false from the real, although he himself had suffered from criticism both in India and abroad. There were many who had first claimed to love him and later had vilified him if their demands were not met. Among such individuals were journalists who, without enquiring, condemned Baba and sought to criticise him. But Baba always observed that if his universal work was to succeed fully and completely, it was imperative that he be faced with opposition. [46] In fact, often when Baba was accused he would ask his lovers not to be angry or violent. On the contrary he blessed those who had opposed him, in the same way as Jesus did when he said from the Cross, "Father, forgive them for they know not what they do."

When India's Prime Minister, Jawaharlal Nehru, died in the summer of 1964, Baba remarked, "Jawaharlal Nehru was matchless as a statesman and India will have to wait another seven-hundred years to find another jewel like him; he can be said to have been a Karma Yogi. Only when I come again through my next advent on earth will there be another like Jawaharlal."

[46] Baba gave darshan to his lovers May 1 – 6, 1965. On May 3, during the darshan hour, a lover asked Baba, "How is the pain in your neck?" Baba replied, "Infinite. It is both physical and universal. When I break my silence, it will vanish." Someone else queried, "When will you break your silence?" Baba said, "I am also eager to break my silence, and then I shall also be free of oppression. My observing silence for so many years is not for nothing. When I break my silence, the impact will be universal. No one knows how I am suffering. My suffering is not only physical but also mental and spiritual. There is a great difference between your mental and spiritual suffering and mine. My mental suffering is very intense and is because of the pseudo saints that abound in the world today. My spiritual suffering is because I know I am free in myself but bound in you."

His Will

In December Baba's youngest brother, Adi S. Irani, who lives in England, visited him with his family. It is on record that on this occasion it was astonishing to witness the tremendous awareness of seven-year-old Shireen, Baba's niece.

When Baba told her that he loved her, she went over and said in his ear: "I love you even more."

Shireen asked several intelligent questions which intrigued all those around her.

"Baba, I know we are born again and again, but you are God so how is it that you get born?"

Baba replied, "Once in a while God takes birth because of his Love for His Creation. I am born in human form so that you may see me as you are, and if you are fortunate to know me and love me then some day you will see me as I really am."

Shireen shot back, "You are in all of us, then are we all in you, Baba?"

Baba nodded, "Yes, that is so."

"We are your children, then why can't we stay with you?"

Baba very lovingly replied, "If you love me, then I am with you wherever you are staying."

A very puzzled Shireen asked, "If I did not love you, Baba — oh, I am not saying I don't, because I do love you! — But just supposing I didn't, then it would not be my fault, would it, Baba? It would be because you did not want me to love you?"

Baba said, "Yes, it is all my Will. My will governs the creation. You love me because I want you to love me."

Shireen then asked the last question, "You are beautiful and so merciful, then why did you create snakes and scorpions?"

"You, Shireen, are so pretty and sweet, yet when you sit on the potty you bring out what is dirty and stinking. Why do you do it? Because it is necessary — and moreover it keeps you well and pretty. And so are all things in God's creation necessary. Both good and bad are mine."

47 After the week-long darshan programme, Baba gave me personal
interviews for three days. Baba
enthusiastically approved of my
suggestion to publish a magazine
devoted to him and his work. The
accepted title was THE GLOW.
Baba called this magazine "my
child" and asked me to nurture it
with love and care. The first issue
of THE GLOW appeared in February
1966 with a message from Baba:
"I am the Sun which is hidden by
the shadow of yourself. Cease
thinking that you are your shadow,
and you will find that the Sun which
I am is your own Reality." Another
message in the same issue: "Be
composed in the Reality of my Love
for all confusion and despair is
your own shadow which will vanish
when I speak the Word."

Naosherwan

In May 1965 Baba held a mass darshan in Poona where thousands
came for his sahavas. His message this time had a different note:
"All these years I used to embrace you, my lovers, and bow down
to your love for me. Now I cannot embrace you, so I allow you to
bow down to my Love for you." During this sahavas Baba told his
lovers that on the occasion of their being with him he did not wish
to give them a lot of words to exercise their minds because he
wanted their minds to sleep so that their hearts might awaken to
his love. "You have had enough of words, I have had enough of
words. It is not through words that I give what I have to give. In
the silence of your perfect surrender, my love which is always
silent can flow to you — to be yours always to keep and to share
with those who seek me. When the Word of my Love breaks out of
its silence and speaks in your hearts, telling you who I really am,
you will know that that is the Real Word you have been always
longing to hear." **47**

Baba addressing his lovers in May 1965 in Poona through Eruch Jessawala, his secretary
and interpreter. It is erroneous to believe that Baba gave the theme of the message or
discourse and it was the interpreter who gave it form. In fact Baba gave out each word in
its proper context and elaborated each message in full.

False Reality

The sahavas for the Westerners scheduled in 1965 was cancelled by Baba because "the world situation is very bad, and growing worse daily. The pressure of my universal work is affecting my health tremendously and the pain in my neck is beyond limit. It is the universal Cross that I bear..." He added, "sometime, somewhere, somehow, I will meet my old and new Western lovers before I break my silence." All of Baba's Western lovers were informed of the cancellation of the sahavas, except one young American, Robert Dreyfuss, who had set out from Boston in September 1965 and had hitch-hiked his way to India, to be on time for Baba's darshan. He reached Meherazad three months later only to be told by the mandali that the sahavas had been cancelled. Baba did not allow the American boy to return disheartened. On the contrary Baba received him and asked him to return to America and persuade the youth of his country to give up drugs. Baba said, "Tell those that are, that if drugs could make one realize God, then God is not worthy of being God. No drugs. Many people in India smoke hashish and ganja — they see colours and forms and lights and it makes them elated. But this elation is only temporary, it is a false experience. It gives only an experience of illusion, and serves to take one farther away from Reality.

"Tell those who indulge in these drugs (LSD, etc.) that it is harmful physically, mentally and spiritually, and that they should stop the taking of these drugs. Your duty is to tell them, regardless of whether they accept what you say or if they ridicule or humiliate you, to boldly and bravely face these things. Leave the results to me; I will help you in my work. You are to bring my message to those ensnared in the drugnet of illusion, that they should abstain, that the drugs will bring more harm than good." [48]

Later, in reply to Richard Alpert, a leading exponent of drug ingestion, Baba said, "No drug, whatever its great promise, can help one to attain the spiritual Goal. There is no short cut to the Goal except through the grace of the Perfect Master; and drugs, LSD more than others, give only a semblance of "spiritual experiences", a glimpse of the false reality." From time to time Meher Baba continued to clarify doubts and mis-

[48] Dr. Allan Cohen, who started work with the psychedelic guru Timothy Leary, was later disillusioned with drugs and dedicated himself to the dissemination of Meher Baba's messages of 'No Drugs.' Seeking clarification relating to the LSD controversy raging in the U.S., Dr. Cohen posed several questions to Meher Baba.

Baba from his seclusion answered:

* The user of LSD drug could never reach subtle consciousness in this incarnation despite its repeated use, unless the person surrendered to a Perfect Master. To experience real spiritual consciousness, surrenderance to a Perfect Master is necessary.

* The experiences gained through LSD are, in some cases, experiences of the shadows of the subtle plane in the gross world. These experiences have nothing at all to do with spiritual advancement.

* Repeated use of LSD leads to insanity which may prove incurable in mental cases, even with LSD treatment.

* Medical use of LSD helps to cure in some cases mental disorders and madness.

* There is no such thing as areas in the brain reserved for subtle consciousness, and the question of LSD affecting them has no meaning.

* When LSD is used for genuine medical purposes, in controlled doses, under the supervision of specialists, there are no chances of brain, liver or kidney being damaged.

* Continued LSD use for non-medical purposes results in madness and death eventually.

givings on the subject of drugs while his anti-drug evangelists spoke to audiences, gave radio and television interviews and set up drug guidance centres.

Baba in Poona in 1965. He was a vegetarian and ate very simple food. His diet was comprised mainly of liquids.

Baba was very fond of tea and did not drink alcohol. He allowed vegetarians to follow their diet and non-vegetarians to eat meat, fish, etc.

Crucifixion

Most of 1966 was spent in seclusion. His health had suffered.
Dr. Ram Ginde, a distinguished doctor of Bombay, who was attending Baba, wrote: "Whatever I know from the knowledge
of his cervical condition, I have tried to do in all sincerity. But
I must admit, as I have admitted before, my utter failure in
regard to relieving Beloved Baba's pain. I plead quite helpless
in treating him who is as powerful as, nay more powerful than,
an ocean and as helpless as a kitten at one and the same time.
I can only ask his forgiveness." When Baba read this he was
deeply touched; he smiled and asked the doctor not to be worried but to remember that he was very dear to him and that the
root cause of his pain was not physical but universal, and that
it would leave him only in his time.

That year Baba's birthday was observed on a grand scale
throughout the world. In a message to THE GLOW Baba said:
"It is easy to love me, because I am Love. But it is difficult
to love me with that love by which I am attained." His birthday
message said: "Births and deaths are illusory phenomena. One
really dies when one is born to live as God, the Eternal who is
beyond both birth and death." **49**

The Principal of St. Vincent's High School, Poona, where
Baba was a student once, requested a message on the school's
centenary. Baba sent the following message: "Schools help
sincere students to equip themselves with knowledge and to become worthy citizens of society. And those students are wise
who take full advantage of educational institutions and their
facilities.

"But this knowledge is not the be-all and end-all of learning.
And there comes a time when one longs to reach the Source of
knowledge. The journey to this Source can only be undertaken
when one learns to love in all simplicity and honesty the One
whom the pride of intellect veils."

"When mind soars in pursuit of the things conceived in space,
it pursues emptiness; but when man dives deep within himself,
he experiences the fullness of existence."

A circular sent in March 1968 came as a surprise to Baba-
lovers all over. It said: "I want all my lovers to know that my
seclusion will not end on March 25, 1968. My seclusion will
have to be prolonged for two months because the work that I

49 Film-Maker Louis Van Gasteren:
Who are you?
Meher Baba: I am God in human
form — but there are many who call
themselves God-incarnate. They
are hypocrites. Better are those
who do not aspire to God-realization. Then there are others who use
hallucinogenic and narcotic drugs
including ganja, charas and bhang.
Apparently uplifted for a while,
they feel other than what they are.
In the end some go crazy. Under
the influence of drugs there are
some who even assert that they have
attained Godhood! It is all hallu-
cination. False experience is never
continuous. Real experience only
is continuous.

am doing in seclusion could not be completed before May 21, 1968. My seclusion which was to end on March 25, 1968, will therefore have to continue until May 21, 1968. This is unavoidable.

"None can have the least idea of the intensity of the work that I am doing in this seclusion. The only hint I can give is that compared with the work I do in seclusion all the important work of the world put together is completely insignificant. Although for me the burden of my work is crushing, the result of my work will be intensely felt by all people in the world." Baba reassured his lovers that the fate of the universe hung on his seclusion and the redemption of mankind depended on his manifestation. He asked his lovers to recite the Master's Prayer and the Prayer of Repentance daily and to observe silence for twenty-four hours on May 19, 1968.

Baba had said something great would happen that had never happened before. He later added, "That which is to happen after 21st May 1968 will be something great, something that has never happened before, something that will not happen again for billions and billions of years." It would happen all of a sudden, not in developing stages.

Baba-lovers the world over yearned for his sahavas and darshan. Men, women and children longed to be in his presence; separation from him had become unbearable for many. They longed to see him and many travelled long distances only to come to the gates where he lived and returned without seeing him because that was the Master's wish. He was in strict seclusion and would not give darshan. Baba told them, "Be patient. Wait in my Love. Those who wait for me never wait in vain. You will see me, but wait till I call. Hold on to my daaman — and wait for my call."

Exclusion

May 21, 1968. The end of Baba's "seclusion" (when he had secluded himself from his lovers) and the beginning of a period referred to as "exclusion" (when even his lovers were excluded from seeing him).[50] Next would come the period of "inclusion" (the time that would include all to his darshan). On the evening of July 30, 1968, Baba declared: "My work is done. It is completed 100 per cent to my satisfaction. The result of this work will also be 100 per cent and will manifest from the end of September." One morning Baba said: "God always existed/God will always exist/He is never changing, ever the same/And Illusion is his Eternal Game." In August of the same year, Baba uttered another cryptic remark, "ever-lasting, never ending/never changing, ever the same/and his oneness in its fullness/plays in manyness His game."

In response to persistent queries of his lovers, Baba decided to give darshan from April 10 to June 10, 1969 in Poona. Baba told them, "No doubt, you people and my lovers everywhere have been wondering why, when my period of intense work in seclusion has finished, I have still not allowed my lovers to see me.

"The strain of that eighteen months' work was tremendous. I used to sit alone in my room for some hours each day while complete silence was imposed on the mandali and no one of them was permitted to enter the room, during those hours every day. The strain was not in the work itself although I was working on all planes of consciousness but in keeping my link with the gross plane. To keep this link I had to continuously hammer my right thigh with my fist. Now, although my health is good, and I would like to fulfill immediately the longing of my lovers to come to me — many to see me for the first time — it will yet take sometime for all traces of the strain to disappear and for me to be 100 per cent fit to see them all; and so because of this, and for practical considerations also, I have decided to give my darshan only to my lovers but not to the general public.

"This is the time for my lovers. The time for the world's crowds to come to me will be when I break my Silence and Manifest my Divinity..."

[50] Despite the strict seclusion, "Meher Baba's message carriers, his 'workers,' starting out in handfuls are now moving on in landfuls." Baba's word spread from land to land like a forest fire setting innumerable hearts aflame. There were thousands who yearned for his touch, longed for a glimpse, and yet during the period of "exclusion" they waited patiently. The conviction of Baba's Avatarhood was so strong and intense that even the newly-born lovers of the Beloved took large strides in doing his bidding.

The last photograph of Meher Baba, taken on December 23, 1968.

51 "I am not limited by this form. I use it like a garment to make my-self visible to you; and I communi-cate with you through words best fitted to your understanding. If I used the language of my own con-sciousness you would not know what I was talking about. Don't try to understand me. My depth is un-fathomable. Just love me. I eter-nally enjoy the Christ state of consciousness and when I speak I shall manifest my true Self; besides giving a general push to the whole world, I shall lead all those who come to me towards Light and Truth."

Meher Baba

Baba later remarked: "I have been saying: the Time is near, it is fast approaching, it is close at hand. Today I say: the Time has come. Remember this!" In mid-January 1969 another circular was issued, part of which read: "With the present condition of health, how Beloved Baba will give darshan to thousands who will come, yet remains to be determined; but it will be. He will give his darshan. This darshan, Baba says, will be the last given in Silence — the last before he speaks his world-renewing Word of words."

Before long, things started happening in quick succession. In a letter written on January 26, 1969, Mani Irani quoted Meher Baba's message on his seventy-fifth birthday, issued earlier. It said: "To love me for what I may give you is not loving me at all. To sacrifice anything in my cause to gain something for yourself is like a blind man sacrificing his eyes for sight. I am the Divine Beloved, worthy of being loved because I am Love. He who loves me because of this will be blessed with unlimited sight and will see me as I am." **51**

The Eternal Beloved

In the latter half of January, Baba's health started deteriorating fast. His physical suffering and pain had become more and more evident. On January 30 Baba's body shook with severe spasms. Dr. Grant was called from Poona and Dr. Ram Ginde from Bombay to Meherazad. Just before Dr. Grant left, Baba told him, "My time has come." Surprisingly, Mohammad, the mast living at lower Meherabad, uttered in a rambling lisp, "Tomorrow (January 31) Dada (Baba) is coming here and is going to join Gustadji (one of the mandali members who had passed away some years earlier)."

In the early hours of Friday, January 31, 1969, Baba instructed Aloba (one of the mandali members) to bring a board at 10 in the morning from the mandali hall to be kept in Baba's room. On the board three couplets of the poet Hafiz were written:

1) "Befitting a fortunate slave, carry out every command of the Master, without any question of 'why' and 'what.'"

2) "About what you hear from the Master, never say it is wrong, because, my dear, the fault lies in your own incapacity to understand Him."

3) "I am the slave of the Master who has released me from ignorance; whatever my Master does is of the highest benefit to all concerned."

The spasms continued and his body shook intensely with pain. The allopathic medicines given to him brought no relief. Biochemic pills were administered. Just after twelve noon, when the fourth dose of pills were given, and the resident Dr. Goher gave him an injection, Baba said, "Do not forget that I am God." At 12:15 p.m. Baba's entire physical framework shook with severe spasms as he sat on a surgical bed with his back and head raised. His arms flexed and his mouth closed tight. His respiration suddenly stopped. Baba became motionless. Eruch Jessawala opened Baba's mouth, put his mouth against it and began breathing into his lungs forcibly. This mouth to mouth resuscitation was carried on for thirty minutes. Eruch collapsed on the floor out of sheer exhaustion while Dr. Brieseman from Ahmednagar, who had just arrived with Dr. Ginde and Dr. Donkin, gave him a cardiac massage. Three doctors, Dr. Brieseman, Dr. Donkin and Dr. Ginde examined Baba's heart. Dr. Ginde checked Baba's eye reflexes. It was pronounced that life was extinct. The Avatar had dropped his body. **52**

52 I am now infinitely enjoying bliss and infinitely suffering at the same time. As soon as I drop my body, I will go to my abode of Infinite Bliss.
Meher Baba
September 17, 1954

I am the Ancient One, and you will all love me more and more after my body is dropped, and will see me as I really am.
Meher Baba
September 24, 1954

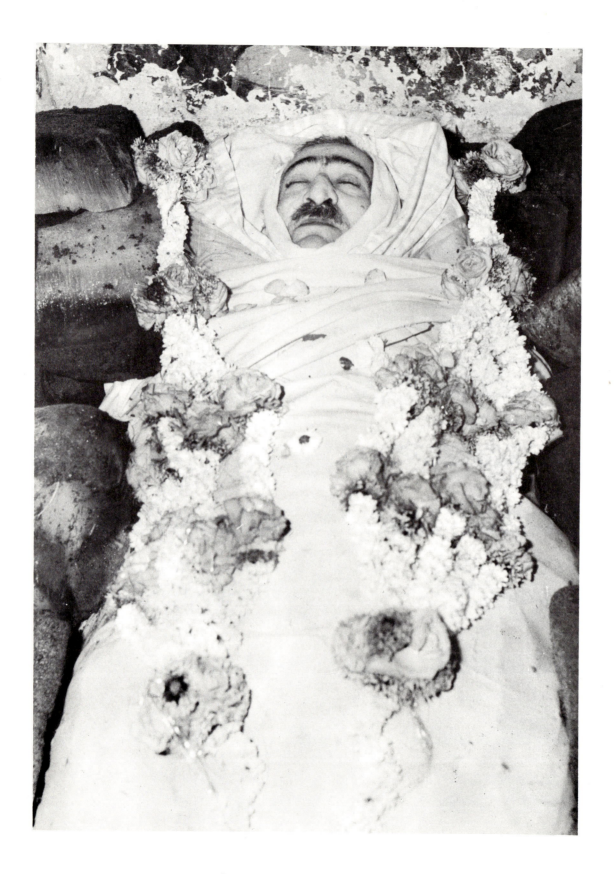

منزل نچون چپرادم که بنده مقبل ‌‌ قبول که : زبان بر سخن که سلطان گفت

BEFITTING A FORTUNATE SLAVE CARRY OUT EVERY COMMAND OF THE **M**ASTER WITHOUT ANY QUESTION OF WHY AND WHAT.

په بشنوی سخن املل مکوکه خطاآت • سخن شناس نئی دلبر اخطا این خیاست

ABOUT WHAT YOU HEAR FROM THE **M**ASTER NEVER SAY IT IS WRONG BECAUSE MY DEAR. THE FAULT LIES IN YOUR OWN INCAPACITY TO UNDERSTAND **H**IM.

بنده کوپیر مغانم که ز جسلم بربا ند ‌ پیر ماهر چه کند عین رعایت باشد

I AM SLAVE OF THE **M**ASTER. **W**HO HAS RELEASED ME FROM IGNORANCE. **W**HATEVER MY **M**ASTER DOES IS OF THE HIGHEST BENEFIT TO ALL CONCERNED. حافظ —**HAFIZ**

(Left) February 1, 1969. Meher Baba's body in the crypt on Meherabad Hill, Ahmednagar, India.

For seven days Baba's body was kept in the tomb at Meherabad hill for thousands of his lovers to take his darshan. Men, women and children, the rich and the poor, Easterners and Westerners, people from all castes, creeds and religions, irrespective of any inconvenience, converged atop Meherabad hill to see and feel their "crucified" Beloved.

The entire area around the hill was virtually a sea of solemn faces mourning their Beloved. Meher Baba was interred on the seventh day.

To honour their Beloved's invitation to take his darshan "sometime, somewhere, somehow" thousands of his lovers from the East and the West poured into Poona in May-June, 1969. Unparalleled in spiritual history, this darshan too was unique when even those who had not seen or met Meher Baba in his physical form, bowed down in their love for him. And that was the beginning of a New Era — an era of continued love and service to the God-Man.

APPENDIX

MEHER BABA'S CALL

Age after age, when the wick of Righteousness burns low, the Avatar comes yet once again to rekindle the torch of Love and Truth. Age after age, amidst the clamor of disruptions, wars, fear and chaos, rings the Avatar's call:

"COME ALL UNTO ME."

Although, because of the veil of illusion, this Call of the Ancient One may appear as a voice in the wilderness, its echo and re-echo nevertheless pervades through time and space to rouse at first a few, and eventually millions, from their deep slumber of ignorance. And in the midst of illusion, as the Voice behind all voices, it awakens humanity to bear witness to the Manifestation of God amidst mankind.

The time is come. I repeat the Call, and bid all come unto me.

This time-honored Call of mine thrills the hearts of those who have patiently endured all in their love for God, loving God only for love of God. There are those who fear and shudder at its reverberations and would flee or resist. And there are yet others who, baffled, fail to understand why the Highest of the High, who is all-sufficient, need necessarily give this Call to humanity.

Irrespective of doubts and convictions, and for the Infinite Love I bear for one and all, I continue to come as the Avatar, to be judged time and again by humanity in its ignorance, in order to help man distinguish the Real from the false.

Invariably muffled in the cloak of the infinitely true humility of the Ancient One, the Divine Call is at first little heeded, until, in its infinite strength, it spreads in volume to reverberate and keep on reverberating in countless hearts as the Voice of Reality.

Strength begets humility, whereas modesty bespeaks weakness. Only he who is truly great can *be* really humble.

When, in the firm knowledge of it, a man admits his true greatness, it is in itself an expression of humility. He accepts his greatness as most natural and is expressing merely what he is, just as a man would not hesitate to admit to himself and others the fact of his being man.

For a truly great man, who knows himself to be truly great, to deny his greatness would be to belittle what he indubitably is. For whereas modesty is the basis of guise, true greatness is free from camouflage.

On the other hand, when a man expresses a greatness he knows or feels he does not possess, he is the greatest hypocrite.

Honest is the man who is not great and, knowing and feeling this, firmly and frankly states that he is not great.

There are more than a few who are not great, yet assume a humility in the genuine belief of their own worth. Through words and actions they express repeatedly their humbleness, professing to be servants of humanity. True humility is not acquired by merely donning a garb of humility. True humility spontaneously and continually emanates from the strength of the truly great. Voicing one's humbleness does not make one humble. For all that a parrot may utter, "I am a man," it does not make it so.

Better the absence of greatness than the establishing of a false greatness by assumed humility. Not only do these efforts at humility on man's part not express strength, they are, on the contrary, expressions of modesty born of weakness, which springs from a lack of knowledge of the truth of Reality.

Beware of modesty. Modesty, under the cloak of humility, invariably leads one into the clutches of self-deception. Modesty breeds egoism, and man eventually succumbs to pride through assumed humility.

The greatest greatness and the greatest humility go hand in hand naturally and without effort.

When the Greatest of all says, "I am the Greatest," it is but a spontaneous expression of an infallible Truth. The strength of his greatness lies not in raising the dead, but in his great humiliation when he allows himself to be ridiculed, persecuted, and crucified at the hands of those who are weak in flesh and spirit. Throughout the ages, humanity has failed to fathom the true depth of the Humility underlying the greatness of the Avatar, gauging his Divinity by its acquired, limited religious standards. Even real saints and sages, who have some knowledge of the Truth, have failed to understand the Avatar's greatness when faced with his real humility.

Age after age, history repeats itself when men and women, in their ignorance, limitations and pride, sit in judgment over the God-incarnated man who declares his Godhood, and condemn him for uttering the Truths they cannot understand. He is indifferent to abuse and persecution for, in his true compassion he understands, in his continual experience of Reality he knows, and in his infinite mercy he forgives.

God is all. God knows all, and God does all. When the Avatar proclaims he is the Ancient One, it is God who proclaims his manifestation on earth. When man utters for or against the Avatarhood, it is God who speaks through him. It is God alone who declares Himself through the Avatar and mankind.

I tell you all, with my Divine Authority, that you and I are not "WE," but "ONE." You unconsciously feel my Avatarhood within you; I consciously feel in you what each of you feel. Thus every one of us is Avatar, in the sense that everyone and everything is everyone and everything, at the same time, and for all time.

There is nothing but God. He is the only Reality, and we all are one in the indivisible Oneness of this absolute Reality. When the One who has realized God says, "I am God. You are God, and we are all one," and also awakens this feeling of Oneness in his illusion-bound selves, then the question of the lowly and the great, the poor and the rich, the humble and the modest, the good and the bad, simply vanishes. It is his false awareness of duality that misleads man into making illusory distinctions and filing them into separate categories.

I repeat and emphasize that, in my continual and eternal experience of Reality, no difference exists between the worldly rich and the poor. But if ever such a question of difference between opulence and poverty were to exist for me, I would deem him really poor who, possessing worldly riches, possesses not the wealth of love for God. And I would know him truly rich who, owning nothing, possesses the priceless treasure of his love for God. His is the poverty that kings could envy and that makes even the King of kings his slave.

Know, therefore, that in the eyes of God the only difference between the rich and the poor is not of wealth and poverty, but in the degrees of intensity and sincerity in the longing for God.

Love for God alone can annihilate the falsity of the limited ego, the basis of life ephemeral. It alone can make one realize the Reality of one's Unlimited Ego, the basis of Eternal Existence. The divine Ego, as the basis of Eternal Existence, continually expresses itself; but shrouded in the veil of ignorance, man misconstrues his Indivisible Ego and experiences and expresses it as the limited, separate ego.

Pay heed when I say with my Divine Authority that the Oneness of Reality is so uncompromisingly unlimited and all-pervading that not only "We are One," but even this collective term of "We" has no place in the Infinite Indivisible Oneness.

Awaken from your ignorance and try at least to understand that, in the uncompromisingly Indivisible Oneness, not only is the Avatar God, but also the ant and the sparrow, just as one and all of you are nothing but God. The only apparent difference is in the states of consciousness. The Avatar knows that that which is a sparrow is not a sparrow, whereas the sparrow does not realize this and, being ignorant of its ignorance, identifies itself as a sparrow.

Live not in ignorance. Do not waste your precious life-span in differentiating and judging your fellowmen, but learn to long for the love of God. Even in the midst of your worldly activities, live only to find and realize your true Identity with your Beloved God.

Be pure and simple, and love all because all are one. Live a sincere life; be natural, and be honest with yourself.

Honesty will guard you against false modesty and will give you the strength of true humility. Spare no pains to help others. Seek no other reward than the gift of Divine Love. Yearn for this gift sincerely and intensely, and I promise in the name of my Divine Honesty that I will give you much more than you yearn for.

I give you all my blessing that the spark of my Divine Love may implant in your hearts the deep longing for love of God.

Reprinted by permission of Universal Spiritual League in America, Inc.
© 1954 by Universal Spiritual League in America, Inc.

THE HIGHEST OF THE HIGH

Consciously or unconsciously, directly or indirectly, each and every creature, each and every human being strives to assert individuality. When eventually man consciously experiences that he is Infinite, Eternal and Indivisible, he is fully conscious of his individuality as God, and experiences Infinite Knowledge, Infinite Power and Infinite Bliss. Thus Man becomes God, and is recognized as a Perfect Master, *Sadguru,* or *Qutub.*

When God manifests on earth in the form of man and reveals his Divinity to mankind, he is recognized as the Avatar—thus God becomes Man. . .

The Avatar is always one and the same, because God is always One and the Same, the Eternal, Indivisible, Infinite One, who manifests himself in the form of man as the Avatar, as the Messiah, as the Prophet, as the Ancient One—the Highest of the High. This Eternally One and the Same Avatar repeats his manifestation from time to time, in different cycles, adopting different human forms and different names, in different places, to reveal Truth in different garbs and different languages, in order to raise humanity from the pit of ignorance and free it from the bondage of delusions.

Of the most recognized and much worshipped manifestations of God as Avatar, that of Zoroaster is the earlier—having been before Rama, Krishna, Buddha, Jesus and Muhammad. Thousands of years ago, he gave to the world the essence of Truth in the form of three fundamental precepts—Good Thoughts, Good Words, and Good Deeds. These precepts were and are constantly unfolded to humanity in one form or another, directly or indirectly in every cycle, by the Avatar of the Age, as he leads humanity towards the Truth. To put these precepts of Good Thoughts, Good Words and Good Deeds into practice is not easily done, though it is not impossible. But to live up to these precepts honestly and literally is apparently as impossible as it is to practice a living death in the midst of life.

In the world there are countless *sadhus, mahatmas, mahapurushas,* saints, yogis and *walis,* though the number of genuine ones is very, very limited. The few genuine ones are, according to their spiritual status, in a category of their own, which is neither on a level with the ordinary human being nor on a level with the state of the Highest of the High.

I am neither a *mahatma* nor a *mahapurush,* neither a *sadhu* nor a saint, neither a yogi nor a *wali.* Those who approach me with the desire to gain wealth or to retain their possessions, those who seek through me relief from distress and suffering, those who ask my help to fulfill and satisfy mundane desires, to them I once again declare that, as I am not a *sadhu,* a saint or a *mahatma, mahapurush* or yogi, to seek these things through me is but to court utter disappointment, though only apparently; for eventually the disappointment is itself instrumental in bringing about the complete transformation of mundane wants and desires.

The *sadhus,* saints, yogis, *walis* and such others who are on the *via media* can and do perform miracles and satisfy the transient material needs of individuals who approach them for help and relief.

The question therefore arises that if I am not a *sadhu,* not a saint, not a yogi, not a *mahapurush* nor a *wali,* then what am I? The natural assumption would be that I am either just an ordinary human being, or I am the Highest of the High. But one thing I say definitely, and that is that I can never be included amongst those having the intermediary status of the real *sadhus,* saints, yogis, and such others.

Now, if I am just an ordinary man, my capabilities and powers are limited—I am no better or different from an ordinary human being. If people take me as such, they should not expect supernatural help from me in the form of miracles or spiritual guidance; and to approach me to fulfill their desires would also be absolutely futile.

On the other hand, if I am beyond the level of an ordinary human being, and much beyond the level of saints and yogis, then I must be the Highest of the High. In which case, to judge me with your human intellect and limited mind and to approach me with mundane desires would not only be the height of folly but sheer ignorance as well; because no amount of intellectual effort could ever understand my ways or judge my Infinite State.

If I am the Highest of the High, my Will is Law, my wish governs the Law, and my Love sustains the Universe. Whatever your apparent calamities and transient sufferings, they are but the outcome of my Love for the ultimate good. Therefore, to approach me for deliverance from your predicaments, to expect me to satisfy your worldly desires, would be asking me to undo what I have already ordained.

If you truly and in all faith accept your Baba as the Highest of the High, it behooves you to lay down your life at his feet, rather than to crave the fulfilment of your desires. Not your one life but your millions of lives would be but a small sacrifice to place at the feet of One such as Baba, who is the Highest of the High; for Baba's unbounded love is the only sure and unfailing guide to lead you safely through the innumerable blind alleys of your transient life.

They cannot obligate me who, surrendering their all—(body, mind, possessions)—which perforce they must discard one day—surrender with a motive; surrender because they understand that to gain the everlasting treasure of Bliss they must relinquish ephemeral possessions. This desire for greater gain is still clinging behind their surrender, and as such the surrender cannot be complete.

Know you all that if I am the Highest of the High, my role demands that I strip you of all your possessions and wants, consume all your desires and make you desireless rather than satisfy your desires. *Sadhus,* saints, yogis and *walis* can give you what you want; but I take away your wants and free you from attachments and liberate you from the bondage of ignorance. I am the One to take, not the One to give what you want or as you want.

Mere intellectuals can never understand me through their intellect. If I am the Highest of the High, it becomes impossible for the mind to gauge me, nor is it possible for my ways to be fathomed by the human mind.

I am not to be attained by those who, loving me, stand reverently by in rapt admiration. I am not for those who ridicule me and point at me with contempt. To have a crowd of tens of millions flocking around me is not what I am for. I am for the few who, scattered amongst the crowd, silently and unostentatiously surrender their all— body, mind and possessions—to me. I am still more for those who, after surrendering their all, never give another thought to their surrender. They are all mine who are prepared to renounce even the very thought of their renunciation and who, keeping constant vigil in the midst of intense activity, await their turn to lay down their lives for the cause of Truth at a glance or sign from me. Those who have indomitable courage to face willingly and cheerfully the worst calamities, who have unshakable faith in me, eager to fulfill my slightest wish at the cost of their happiness and comfort, they indeed truly love me.

From my point of view, far more blessed is the atheist who confidently discharges his worldly responsibilities, accepting them as his honorable duty, than the man who presumes he is a devout believer in God, yet shirks the responsibilities apportioned to him through Divine Law and runs after sadhus, saints and yogis, seeking relief from the suffering which ultimately would have pronounced his eternal liberation.

To have one eye glued on the enchanting pleasures of the flesh and with the other expect to see a spark of Eternal Bliss is not only impossible but the height of hypocrisy.

I cannot expect you to understand all at once what I want you to know. It is for me to awaken you from time to time throughout the ages, sowing the seed in your limited minds, which must in due course and with proper heed and care on your part, germinate, flourish, and bear the fruit of that True Knowledge which is inherently yours to gain.

If, on the other hand, led by your ignorance you persist in going your own way, none can stop you in your choice of progress; for that too is progress which, however slow and painful, eventually and after innumerable reincarnations, is bound to make you realize that which I want you to know *now*. To save yourself from further entanglement in the maze of delusion and self-created suffering which owes its magnitude to the extent of your ignorance of the true Goal, *awake now*. Pay heed and strive for Freedom by experiencing ignorance in its true perspective. Be honest with yourself and God. One may fool the world and one's neighbors, but one can never escape from the knowledge of the omniscient—such is the Divine Law.

I declare to all of you who approach me, and to those of you who desire to approach me, accepting me as the Highest of the High, that you must never come with the desire in your heart which craves for wealth and worldly gain, but only with the fervent longing to give your all—body, mind and possessions—with all their attachments. Seek me not to extricate you from your predicaments, but find me to surrender yourself wholeheartedly to my Will. Cling to me not for worldly happiness and short-lived comforts, but adhere to me through thick and thin, sacrificing your own happiness and comforts at my feet. Let my happiness be your cheer and my comfort your rest. Do not ask me to bless you with a good job, but desire to serve me more diligently and honestly without expectation of reward. Never beg of me to save your life or the lives of your dear ones, but beg of me to accept you and permit you to lay down your life for me. Never expect me to cure you of your bodily afflictions, but beseech me to cure you of your ignorance. Never stretch out your hands to receive anything from me, but hold them high in praise of me whom you have approached as the Highest of the High.

If I am then the Highest of the High, nothing is impossible to me; and though I do not perform miracles to satisfy individual needs—the satisfaction of which would result in entangling the individual more and more in the net of ephemeral existence—yet time and again at certain periods I manifest the Infinite Power in the form of miracles, but only for the spiritual upliftment and benefit of humanity and all creatures.

However, miraculous experiences have often been experienced by individuals who love me and have unswerving faith in me, and these have been attributed to my *nazar* or Grace on them. But I want all to know that it does not befit my lovers to attribute such individual miraculous experiences to my state of the Highest of the High. If I am the Highest of the High, I am above these illusory plays of *maya* in the course of the Divine Law. Therefore, whatever miraculous experiences are experienced by my lovers who recognize me as such, or by those who love me unknowingly through other channels, they are but the outcome of their own firm faith in me. Their unshakable faith often superseding the course of the play of *maya* gives them those experiences which they call miracles. Such experiences derived through firm faith eventually do good and do not entangle the individuals who experience them in further and greater bindings of Illusion.

If I am the Highest of the High, then a wish of my Universal Will is sufficient to give, in an instant, God-realization to one and all, and thus free every creature in creation from the shackles of Ignorance. But blessed is Knowledge that is gained through the experience of Ignorance, in accordance with the Divine Law. This knowledge is made possible for you to attain in the midst of Ignorance by the guidance of Perfect Masters and surrender to the Highest of the High.

Reprinted by permission from *The God-Man*
© 1964 by C. B. Purdom

WHAT BABA MEANS BY REAL WORK

Addressing a large gathering of his devotees and workers, Meher Baba said:

This is no political or social meeting. The meeting for which you all have assembled here, and which is the first of its kind that I have held in these sixty years of my life, is for the Divine Cause. This assemblage reminds me of former meetings during my previous Incarnations. Then the circumstances were different; but since eternity the same God-Incarnate has been presiding over such meetings for the same Cause—the Divine Cause. Thus never has it been more truly said than in the spiritual cause that history repeats itself.

Even if this meeting were to take all night for what I have to say, I would not mind, because this one night would be worth millions of nights if you all honestly live up to and act according to what I wish for my real workers. The Apostles and the 'Asahaba' who worked for the Divine Cause did my work at the very cost of life itself. So heed my words most attentively.

My personally contacting the masses in India through vast 'darshan programmes' has been sufficient for my work. The presentation of addresses and the giving of messages mean nothing on the actual Spiritual Path. I tell you with my Divine Authority that chanting my 'arti,' performing my 'puja,' garlanding me, offering me fruits and sweets and bowing down to me, in themselves, mean absolutely nothing. It is a waste of money to spend on garlands, fruits and sweets as offerings to me for the conventional 'puja,' and a sheer waste of breath and energy to merely chant my 'arti.' From time eternal, gods have been performing my real 'puja.' **What I want from all my lovers is real, unadulterated love, and from my genuine workers I expect real work done.**

I want also to draw your attention to the fact that miracles experienced by my devotees and admirers, both in the East and in the West, have been attributed to me. On the basis of my Divine Honesty I tell you that in this Incarnation I have not, up till now, consciously performed a single miracle. Whenever a miracle has been attributed to me, it has always been news to me. What I wish to emphasize is that by attributing such miracles to me, people cheapen and lower my status as the Highest of the High. But today I do say this, that the moment I break my silence and utter the Original Word, the first and last miracle of 'BABA' will be performed. And when I perform that Miracle, I shall not raise the dead, but shall make those who live for the world dead to the world and live in God. I shall not give sight to the blind, but make people blind to illusion and make them see God as Reality.

I have had enough of this alphabet board and my silence. I must break my silence soon. And when I do, all will come to know of it. Those who have come in contact with me will have a glimpse of Me. Some will have a little, some a little more, and some still more. When the 'Power House' is switched on, there will be Light wherever the electric bulbs are connected with it, provided these bulbs are not fused. Where the bulbs are of small candle power, the light will be little; where the bulbs are of high candle power, the light will be considerable. Where a bulb is fused, there will be no light.

Love me wholeheartedly. The time for the Power House to be switched on is so near that the only thing which will count **now** is Love. That is why I have been telling you all to love me more and more. Love me, love me, love me, and then you will find me.

From you I want no surrender, no mind, no body, no possessions, only LOVE.

I come now to the main point of **'Baba's work and workers.'** Those who have assembled here have been called workers of Baba; therefore, you must necessarily first understand what my work is.

I know that you all, big and small, rich and poor, have done your best to work for the Divine Cause. And I say with happiness that you have tried to express your love for me by spreading my messages of Love to the masses. But I feel that something deep down is very wrong, and that you have not clearly understood how my work should be approached. It is natural that amongst workers of any cause, be it political, social or spiritual, there are bound to be differences of opinion. These differences of opinion and feelings of competition and jealousy lead to the breakdown of the very basis of work.

You have been called upon to do 'Baba's work,' and you have been called 'Baba's workers.' But is it necessary for you to work at all for 'Baba'? If I am the Highest of the High and God-Incarnate, then where is the necessity for me to have workers and to be entangled with Centres and Organizations, mass Darshan programmes, and other channels through which to spread my Message? Can I not, in my own silent way, do the Universal Work. If I am 'Baba,' which definitely I am, then whether the whole world goes against me or worships me, it is all the same to me. If I am not the Infinite One, but am just as one of you, then thousands of centres and programmes in my name would be of no avail.

The reason I have called upon you individually to work for me is so that each one of you may share in the Divine Cause; and these programmes such as mass Darshans are created to give an opportunity for the **expression of individual and collective love.**

Therefore, if you are prepared to share my Universal Work, the work which falls as your share must be done wholeheartedly and honestly. That work is to spread my Message of Love in every corner of the world—all, rich and poor alike—without any distinction as to religion, caste, creed, sect or sex. My Message always has been and always will be of Love Divine—let the world know it. I entrust this share of the Universal Work to my real workers who genuinely desire to serve in the Divine Cause.

I will now explain to you how you should work. First of all, bear in mind that you should not seek appreciation from me or from others. Though this may seem easy, it is very difficult to put into practice. Remember that work in itself is its own appreciation; the moment you seek appreciation the work is undone. Therefore, seek not any appreciation for the work you do for me.

Secondly, do not count upon someone else or on outside help in your work for me. Many of you are ready to work for me one hundred percent; yet because some of you are poor and have families, you cannot devote your time and means for my work. But why then work beyond your means? When the worker depends upon anyone or anything, the work suffers. Therefore do as much as **you** can, but do it honestly.

Thirdly, if money is collected for the work and spent wrongly and without being accounted for, then all work in the name of the Divine Cause must be stopped immediately by the so-called workers. Even one penny extracted in my name without true foundation is dishonesty, and will be the cause of millions of rebirths; and for one cent taken from others by such false pretensions, one dies a million deaths! Therefore, let **honesty in work** prevail.

Fourthly, when you spread my eternal Message of Love to others, show them first that **you** really love me. Do not merely make them read my books and messages; do more. Live such a life of love, sacrifice, forgiveness and tolerance that others will automatically love me. If instead of doing the real work of love you start doing organized propaganda work for me, it is absurd. I need no propaganda or publicity. I do not want propaganda and publicity, but I do want love and honesty. If you cannot live the life of love and honesty, you should stop working for me. I am quite capable of doing my Universal Work alone.

Fifthly, I want you all to know for certain that 'Baba's work' needs no money. In other ages my work has been done without money; it can now be done without money. When money was in use, it was the cause of Judas' undoing, and for which he sold Jesus. It is natural for those workers who are poor to think that they must have money for 'Baba's work' to spread far and wide his Message of Love. But, from my point of view, to **depend** on money for 'Baba's work' is work undone. To ask people to give money and then in return to propagate 'Baba's Message of Love' is utter folly. Therefore, whether you have money or not, let it not affect my work. Money comes and goes; whereas, my work is eternal. Money does not play any important role in my work of the Divine Cause; it is the life that you live that plays the most important role. Hence, **live** such a life that others not only know you love me, but **feel** your love for me. Begin to live this life and let other workers for the Divine Cause follow suit. Let there be no compromise in this; no mixture of honesty and dishonesty. Absolute honesty must be there—there can be no 'Baba' without it. I am Baba—I know what I AM.

All those who love me and want to share my work can do so. Those who have money and can afford to go from place to place can spread my Message of Divine Love in every distant nook and corner. Those who have a little money can go around their own town and district spreading my Message of Love and living the life of love by doing the service of God. And those who have no money, or have families and little time, can also do the work by guiding their own families and friends towards Baba's **Love**. If you all love me even a little, I want your hearts towards each other to be clean and for you to forget your differences. Cleanse your hearts and **live for Baba**.

Outwardly you may establish hundreds of centres for Baba, or none at all; that is your own responsibility. But bear in mind that for my work it is not necessary to have centres, or offices, nor the 'botheration' of accounts and the collecting of money. Let Baba's Love be the Centre, the Office, the Help and the Work.

I want my lovers and workers to know that there is no greater 'Baba's Centre' than the heart of my lover. **Those who truly love me are my Centres in the world.** Let each 'Baba-lover,' wherever he or she may be, be a 'Baba's Centre' personified, radiating the eternal Message of Love Divine, living the life of love, sacrifice and honesty.

When I say that each one of you be a 'Baba-Centre,' it does not mean that each of you should work individually when you can work collectively in groups as 'Baba-Centres.' Neither does this mean that you should not work on your own. I have shown you how I desire the work to be done; it is for you to follow the method best suited to you.

Let me now see how you love and work for 'Baba.' **I am everywhere. I am in you and see you.** Do your share in my work in all sincerity. Be responsible for what you do and how you do it. I now will do my personally ordained work and break my silence very shortly.

I love all. I am the Lord of Love, the slave of my lovers, and devoted to my devotees. Although I do not perform miracles, I will give anything to whomsoever asks for it from the bottom of the heart. If I am 'Baba,' everything is possible to me. Ask wholeheartedly and you will get it from me. But this I tell you too, that **the one who asks for my love will be the chosen one.**

You who love me have expressed your love in a way that touches my heart, and I feel very happy. Yet I have not known one who loves me as I would wish to be loved. There are about 220 men and women from the East and West who have so completely and utterly surrendered to me that they would do anything I say. Whatsoever I order them they will carry out, even if it means being cut to pieces.

To surrender is higher than to love, and paradoxical as it may seem, **to love me as I ought to be loved is impossible, yet to obey me is possible.** Therefore, to say you love me and yet not to obey me would be hypocritical.

The time is very near for the breaking of my silence and then, within a short period all will happen—my humiliation, my glorification, my manifestation, and the dropping of my body. All this will happen soon and within a short period. So, from this moment love me more and more.

Do not propagate what you do not feel. What your heart says and your conscience dictates about me, pour out without hesitation. Be unmindful of whether you are ridiculed or accepted in pouring out your heart for me, or against me, to others.

If you take 'Baba' as 'God-Incarnate,' say so; do not hesitate.

If you think 'Baba' is 'the devil,' say it; do not be afraid.

I am everything that you take me to be, and I am also beyond everything. If your conscience says that 'Baba' is the Avatar, say it even if you are stoned for it. But if you feel he is not, then say that you feel 'Baba' is not the Avatar. Of myself I say again and again, **I am the Ancient One—the Highest of the High.**

If you had even the tiniest glimpse of my Divinity, all doubts would vanish and love—Real Love—would be established. Illusion has such a tight grip on you that you forget Reality. Your life is a Shadow. **The only Reality is Existence Eternal—which is GOD."**

FINAL DECLARATION

I am very happy to have you all here.

I know that very many of you have come to Meherabad under greatly difficult circumstances. Some of you have covered thousands of miles, and even crossed continents to be at Meherabad today. It is your deep love for me that has braved all obstacles and prompted you to sacrifice your comforts and conveniences to honour my call and to be near me today.

I am deeply touched by your devotion and I am proud of the hearts that contain such love and loyalty.

There are many more devoted hearts like yours yearning to be present here, but these are not to be seen in your midst today. I know that in spite of their intense desire to be near me, they could not possibly come for one reason or another. Therefore they depend on you to convey to them in detail all that you see and hear during this two days of unique opportunity that has fallen to your lot. I trust you will not fail them.

Although you are present here with all love and faith in me and though you feel blessed to have my personal contact, yet I know that you will not realize today, as you ought to, the true significance of my call and your presence here at this juncture. Time alone will make most of you realize, not many months from now, the significant importance of this assembly.

The time is fast approaching when all that I have repeatedly stressed, from time to time, will definitely come to pass. Most of you will witness those events, and will recall very vividly all that transpires during these two days of your stay at Meherabad.

I have not come to establish anything new—I have come to put life into the old. I have not come to establish retreats or ashrams. I create them for the purpose of my universal work, only to repeatedly dissolve them once that purpose has been served.

The universe is my ashram, and every heart is my house; but I manifest only in those hearts in which all other than me ceases to live.

When my universal religion of love is on the verge of fading into insignificance, I come to breathe life into it and to do away with the farce of dogmas that defile it in the name of religions and stifle it with ceremonies and rituals.

The present universal confusion and unrest has filled the heart of man with greater lust for power and a greed for wealth and fame, bringing in its wake untold misery, hatred, jealousy, frustration and fear. Suffering in the world is at its height, in spite of all the striving to spread peace and prosperity to bring about lasting happiness.

For man to have a glimpse of lasting happiness he has first to realize that God, being in all, knows all; that God alone acts and reacts through all; that God, in the guise of countless animate and inanimate entities, experiences the innumerably varied phenomena of suffering and happiness, and that God himself undergoes all these illusory happenings. Thus, it is God who has brought suffering in human experience to its height, and God alone who will efface this illusory suffering and bring the illusory happiness to its height.

Whether it manifests as creation or disappears into oneness of reality, whether it is experienced as existing and real or is perceived to be false and non-existent, illusion throughout is illusion. There is no end to it, just as there is no end to imagination.

There are two aspects experienced in illusion—manyness and oneness. While manyness multiplies manyness, oneness goes on magnifying itself. Manyness is the 'religion' of illusion on which illusion thrives.

In the illusory beginning of time, there was no such state of mess in illusion as there is today. When the evolution of consciousness began, there was oneness, in spite of the diversity in illusion. With the growth of consciousness, manyness also went on increasing, until now it is about to overlap the limit. Like the wave that reaches its crest, this height of manyness will dissolve itself and bring about the beginning of oneness in illusion. Suffering at its height will cause the destruction of this climax of manyness in illusion.

The time has come for the pre-ordained destruction of multiple separateness which keeps man from experiencing the feeling of unity and brotherhood. This destruction, which will take place very soon, will cause three-fourths of the world to be destroyed. The remaining one-fourth will be brought together to live a life of concord and mutual understanding, thus establishing a feeling of oneness in all fellow-beings, leading them towards lasting happiness.

Before I break my silence or immediately after it, three-fourths of the world will be destroyed. I shall speak soon to fulfill all that is shortly to come to pass.

To affirm religious faiths, to establish societies, or to hold conferences will never bring about the feeling of unity and oneness in the life of mankind, now completely absorbed in the manyness of illusion. Unity in the midst of diversity can be made to be felt only by touching the very core of the heart. That is the work for which I have come.

I have come to sow the seed of love in your hearts so that, in spite of all superficial diversity which your life in illusion must experience and endure, the feeling of oneness, through love, is brought about amongst all the nations, creeds, sects and castes of the world.

In order to bring this about, I am preparing to break my silence. When I break my silence it will not be to fill your ears with spiritual lectures. I shall speak only one Word, and this Word will penetrate the hearts of all men and make even the sinner feel that he is meant to be a saint, while the saint will know that God is in the sinner as much as he is in himself.

When I speak that Word, I shall lay the foundation for that which is to take place during the next seven hundred years. When I come again after seven hundred years, the evolution of consciousness will have reached such an apex that materialistic tendencies will be automatically transmuted into spiritual longing, and the feeling of equality in spiritual brotherhood will prevail. This means that opulence and poverty, literacy and illiteracy, jealousy and hatred, which are in evidence today in their full measure, will then be dissolved through the feelings of the oneness of all men. Prosperity and happiness will then be at their zenith.

This does not mean that oneness in illusion shall remain so eternally. That is because all this that is, is illusion, and the consciousness of oneness as well as of many-ness in illusion is part of the process of evolution. The time is bound to recur when there will be again the same beginning, growth and culmination of the heights of many-ness and oneness in illusion.

My next advent, after I drop this body, will be after seven hundred years, and that will mark the end and the beginning of a cycle of cycles. All cycles of time in illusion end and begin after 700 to 1,400 years, and there have been and will be millions and billions of such cycles in a cycle of cycles; thus, there is no end to illusion, which always remains illusion.

Age after age I come amidst mankind to maintain my own creation of illusion, thereby also awakening humanity to become aware of it. The framework of illusion is always one and the same, but the designs in illusion are innumerable and ever-changing.

My advent is not to destroy illusion because illusion, as it is, is absolutely nothing. I come to make you become aware of the nothingness of illusion. Through you I auto-matically maintain illusion, which is nothing but the shadow of my infinite self, and through me you automatically discard illusion when you are made aware of its falseness.

My manifestation as the Avatar of the time will be of short duration. This short period will, in quick succession, cover my humiliation, the breaking of my silence, my glorification and my violent physical end. Everlastingly, with all the divine bliss within me, I eternally suffer for one and all—thus I am crucified eternally and continually for all.

During this short period, my Word of words will touch the hearts of all mankind, and spontaneously this divine touch will instill in man the feeling of the oneness of all fellow beings. Gradually, in the course of the next seven hundred years, this feeling will supersede the tendency of separateness and rule over the hearts of all, driving away hatred, jealousy and greed that breed suffering, and happiness will reign.

CLARIFICATION

It is really very difficult for anyone to believe and understand what I say, because none can grasp the meaning underlying my words. It is natural for even my intimate mandali not to understand; but I want you to take everything that I said in Meherabad during the meetings very seriously, because all I said was the truth; they were the words of God, and all the things said must come to pass in exactly the manner described by me.

From the day I declared in Meherabad that there will be the destruction of three-fourths of the world, that a strange disease will attack my body, that I shall suffer humiliation, that I shall break my silence and speak one Word, the Word of words, that there will be my glorification, and that finally I shall drop my body when I shall be stabbed in the back, my lovers and others have been confused, trying to interpret my words in different ways.

Everyone is free to interpret my words in any way they think and feel. But one thing I tell you, that whenever I say a thing, I naturally use my own 'language,' and whatsoever is said by me is truth. But my 'language' is such that none can understand or grasp the underlying meaning of what I say; therefore, when I want to say a thing I have simultaneously to make use of your language also, knowing well that you would understand nothing whatsoever if I were to make use of my 'language' alone.

In order to help you to understand my Final Declaration and to put an end to your confusion and worry, I want you all to know that when you saw me dictate on my alphabet board during the Meetings at Meherabad, and heard about:

(1) A strange disease attacking my body: was said in your language.
(2) The humiliation that I shall suffer: was said in your language.
(3) The breaking of my silence and my uttering the one Word of words: was said in my own 'language' and simultaneously in yours, because when I utter that word, it will be an audible word to you.
(4) My Glorification: was said simultaneously in my 'language' and in yours.
(5) The destruction of three-fourths of the world: was said in my own 'language' alone.
(6) The stab in the back: was said in my own 'language' alone.
(7) The dropping of my body: was said in my own 'language' and simultaneously in yours.

Consequently, whatever is said by me in your language, you are able to understand and know what is said; but that which is said in my own 'language' is impossible for you to understand, however much you may try to interpret the meaning behind my words. Only the fulfillment of events can unfold to you, in due course, the meaning of what is said in my own 'language.' I therefore want you not to worry unnecessarily or be confused. Just believe whatever I say is Truth; and all that I have said in my Final Declaration will come to pass precisely as I have dictated, by the end of April 1955. And the beginning of all that is to happen within the period of these six months will be effected by me from the 1st December 1954.

From that date to the 16th January 1955, all concerned should know that:

(1) Each and all things as intimated, declared, and clarified by me are fixed and ordained fact, and God will see that everything happens and is done as fore-ordained by him.

All that is destined to take place is unavoidable, yet the resultant effects can be modified in two different ways according to circumstances. The modification of the effects of a destined plan can either affect the intensity, scope, shape or size of the chain of events, or bring about a considerable change in the factor of time. In either case, the effects can be modified as much in relation to me and those closely connected with me as to the world at large, For example, the world can absorb fully a simultaneous spiritual and material shock either by a modification in the quality and quantity of events or by a considerable change in the time factor. If the time limit April 1955 as mentioned at the Meherabad Meetings remains unchanged, then in order to enable the world fully to absorb the shock of shocks, the chain of events may be modified both in degree and in kind. But if the time limit is changed considerably, the events will take place without any modification whatsoever.

In that event the most important and significant point is that definitely and emphatically the link between my physical body and all my external activities as carried on up to now will be dropped by April 1955, and there will take place an immeasurable change in the external relations between me and those closely connected with me. If I do not drop my physical body, I shall yet, so to say, 'die,' for I shall then become actually dead to the world up to the end of the modified period of time. During the indefinite period of the modified time, I shall completely stop one and all of my external activities as carried on by me in the course of the different phases of my physical life so far, including the present life of retirement amongst those who live with me permanently.

I shall then, throughout this modified period of time, live a life of complete physical detachment from everything and everybody except a few as will be absolutely necessary for my requirements of nature in the barest sense of living the life of a man alive.

(2) I wish all my lovers to observe a fast and remain only on water (which can be taken any number of times during the fast) for 24 hours, from 8 p.m. on Saturday, February 12th, to 8 p.m. on Sunday, February 13th (local time in each country), and to devote all available time during the twenty-four hours in praying to God in the way each likes best to pray to him.

(3) Honesty is the keynote to Divinity. He who can love God honestly can lose himself in God and find himself as God.

Reprinted by permission from *The God-Man*
© 1964 by C. B. Purdom

REMEMBER ME

Whatever brings you nearer to the path and suits you best is best for you, provided you are able to put it into practice wholeheartedly and in harmony with the natural bent of your mind. A good runner who remains indifferent to racing cannot make good progress, but a lame man who keeps on limping vigorously may soon arrive at the path. If it is not used properly the best car is virtually useless to the traveller, however concerned he may be to arrive at his destination.

I have already told you that love for God and obedience to a master are beyond the reach of man on his own, and that complete surrender is almost impossible for him. The next best thing then is for man to purify his heart. This is also very difficult because every action, whether trivial or important, good or bad, has left its impression on his mind.

Thus every human mind is a gigantic storehouse of accumulated and fast-changing impressions. How can one gain an adequate idea of these impressions left by innumerable actions—and particularly those born of anger, lust and greed—during the lengthy course of the evolution of man's consciousness through the progressive stages of the mineral, vegetable and animal kingdoms of life?

The obvious remedies for this situation are to use no remedies. For example, if one engages in a secluded life of mere physical renunciation, one is more likely to drive underground than eliminate the dirt of impressions from one's mind. Under a false sense of external security born of the secluded life, the mind is apt to become weakened and so stop struggling. Then, instead of achieving freedom from the bindings of impressions, the mind is likely to succumb eventually to its impressions and thus develop greater bindings.

By becoming physically free of the bindings created by the impressions in your mind, you have not rooted them out of your mind. Although your *body* may be temporarily freed, as it is in the sound-sleep state, yet your *mind* remains bound by the impressions. Even when the body itself is dropped you do not become free, for your mind remains bound by the impressions which the mind has created.

Even as the mind cannot be freed of bindings by mere physical renunciation, so the heart cannot be purified by mere mechanical following of the external forms and fads of religion. One must act on principles and not by rituals.

For example, the essence of Zoroaster's teachings lies in the principles of good thoughts, good words and good deeds, and not in the multitude of rituals and ceremonies. These latter serve more as an escape from, rather than as an incentive to, the task of purifying the heart.

In achieving good thoughts, good words and good deeds, one finds that good is not just something better than bad, nor merely the opposite of bad; and not-bad is not necessarily good. 'Good' and 'bad' are terms that reinforce illusory duality more than they remind one of divine unity. From the point of view of truth, thoughts, words and deeds are 'good' only when they are born of the longing for, or the love of, God, the one and only truth.

Although born a Zoroastrian, all religions are the same to me insofar as they help men to come nearer and nearer to God, who is ever most near to man.

It is better not to worship if your heart is not in it. Any prayer made mechanically in a spirit of show or ceremony is all a farce. It results in greater bindings through one's pretense to purity. Similarly, a self-imposed fast, if not observed through a sense of obedience or through love of truth, may make a clock the object of your fast through watching to see when it is time to stop. Such actions tighten more than they loosen the bindings of impressions.

By not eating, you gather the impressions of "not eating." Doing or not doing anything—whether sleeping, staying awake or even breathing—creates impressions on your mind. Therefore, you may fast indefinitely, hang yourself upside down or knock out your brains on a slab of stone, and yet not free your mind of its impressions.

Why, then, should you necessarily give up eating, drinking, doing your duty to your wife and children and looking after the welfare of others? Such duties do not obstruct your way to the path at all. What *do* come in your way are the bindings which you create unnecessarily for yourself through attachment to the objects connected with those duties. You can own the world without being attached to it, so long as you do not allow yourself to be owned by any part of it.

Suppose, for instance, that a man, in spite of doing his best, loses his family and is unable to obtain enough to eat for himself. If he remains unconcerned, this amounts to his having really given up both his family and eating.

A real fast for the mind is to have no thoughts at all, but ordinarily this is impossible. Knowingly or unknowingly, like breathing, thoughts keep coming and going, whether you are dreaming the dream of your life or the dreams in your sleep. You become completely free of thoughts only when you are in the state of sound sleep—the most-original beyond-beyond state of God. But in sound sleep you also lose consciousness. Your mind is then temporarily at rest, but not freed of its impressions.

Let us soon finish these discussions, lest some of you slip right into the most-original state!

The best way to cleanse the heart and prepare for the stilling of the mind is to lead a normal, worldly life. Living in the midst of your day-to-day duties, responsibilities, likes, dislikes, etc., will help you. All these become the very means for the purification of your heart. This natural, normal method depends for its success upon a clear idea of the force behind your thoughts, and the facts underlying your actions.

The force behind your thoughts is the force of the impressions in your mind. The impressions are there due to your own previous actions. Actions are the cause of impressions and thoughts are but the expression of the impressions. This being true, the more you try to check your thoughts, the more you interfere with the natural process of their expression. Sooner or later, with the added force produced by suppression, the impressions are bound to express themselves completely.

The truth of action is that every action, significant or insignificant, voluntary or involuntary, is at once impressed in turn upon your mind. Like a non-greasy stain, a light impression can be easily wiped out, but impressions caused by actions conceived in anger, lust or greed are hard to remove. In short, actions produce impressions, and impressions produce thoughts. Thoughts in turn tend to precipitate further action.

For the purification of your heart, leave your thoughts alone, but maintain a constant vigil over your actions. When you have thoughts of anger, lust or greed, do not worry about them, and do not try to check them. Let all such thoughts come and go without putting them into action. Try to think counter-thoughts in order to discern, to discriminate, to learn, and above all to unlearn the actions which are prompted by your own impressions.

It is better to feel angry sometimes than merely to suppress anger. You then have an opportunity to think about anger, its causes and its consequences. Although your mind may be angry, do not let your heart know it. Remain unaffected.

If you never feel angry, you will be like stone, in which form the mind is least developed. Similarly, if you never have lusty thoughts you cannot achieve the merit of having avoided lustful actions.

Let the thoughts of anger, lust and greed come and go freely and unasked without putting them into words and deeds. Then the related impressions in your mind begin to wear out and become less and less harmful. But when you put such thoughts into action—whether overtly or secretly—you develop new impressions worse than those which are spent in the act. These new impressions root even more firmly in your mind.

The fire of divine love alone can destroy all impressions once and for all. However, remembering me can keep down the impurities in the impressions in your mind, as alum catches hold of (flocculates) dirt in a vessel of turbid water. Therefore, when you feel angry or have lustful thoughts, remember Baba at once. Let my name serve as a net around you so that your thoughts, like mosquitoes, may keep buzzing around you and yet not sting you. In that manner you can prevent unwanted thoughts from turning into unwanted actions, and thus eventually bring your heart to the purification required for me to manifest therein.

But it is not child's play to remember me constantly during your moments of excitement. If, in spite of being very angry, you refrain from expressing anger, it is indeed a great achievement. It means that when your mind becomes angry your heart does not know it, just as when your heart loves me your mind need not know it. In fact, your mind does not know that your heart loves when, prepared to give up life itself, you lead a life of day-to-day obedience and duty.

You can also entrust your mind to me by remembering me or repeating my name in your heart as often as you can. Remember me so often that your mind is at a loss to find other thoughts to feed on.

Although I am "taking" my own name continuously, I have come to hear it repeated by my lovers, and even though I were deaf I would hear it if you repeated it only once with all your heart in it. If you cannot remember me constantly, then always take (repeat, think of) my name before going to sleep and on waking up.

At least remember to remember me when you breathe your last, and you will still come to me. But how will you remember at the last moment, unless you start to remember me right now?

LOVE, LOVER AND BELOVED

To garland me, to bow down to me and to sing my praises are comparatively the three most unimportant things. The three most important things on the path to God-realization are love, obedience and surrender. There is no possibility of compromise about these three.

Love is a gift from God to man, obedience is a gift from master to man, and surrender is a gift from man to master. The one who loves desires to do the will of the beloved, and seeks union with the beloved. Obedience performs the will of the beloved and seeks the pleasure of the beloved. Surrender resigns to the will of the beloved and seeks nothing.

One who loves is the lover of the beloved. One who obeys is the beloved of the beloved. One who surrenders all—body, mind and all else—has no existence other than that of the beloved, who alone exists in him. Therefore, greater than love is obedience, and greater than obedience is surrender. And yet, as words, all three can be summed up in one phrase—love-divine.

One can find volumes and volumes of prose and poetry about love, but there are very, very few persons who have found love and experienced it. No amount of reading, listening, and learning can ever tell you what love is. Regardless of how much I explain love to you, you will understand it less and less if you think you can grasp it through the intellect or imagination . . .

The difference between love and intellect is something like that between night and day; they exist in relation to one another and yet as two different things. Love is real intelligence capable of realizing truth; intellect is best suited to know all about duality, which is born of ignorance and *is* entirely ignorance. When the sun rises, night is transformed into day. Just so, when love manifests, not-knowing (ignorance) is turned into conscious-knowing (knowledge).

In spite of the difference between a keenly intelligent person and a very unintelligent person, each is equally capable of experiencing love. The quality which determines one's capacity for love is not one's wit or wisdom, but one's readiness to lay down life itself for the beloved, and yet remain alive. One must, so to speak, slough off body, energy, mind and all else, and become dust under the feet of the beloved. This dust of a lover who cannot remain alive without God—just as an ordinary man cannot live without breath—is then transformed into the beloved. Thus man becomes God.

Listen to love without philosophizing about it. None present here loves me as I ought to be loved. If all of you had such love, none of you would be left before me. You would all have realized God and we would all have become the One which we all are in reality and in eternity.

You accept me as being simultaneously God and man, the highest of the high and the lowest of the low; but by *accepting* me to be THAT, you do not *know* me to be THAT. To know me as I am, you must become conscious of my *real state,* and for that you must love me as I love you.

The mandali who have been with me through thick and thin all these years are fully prepared for love of me to lay down their very lives at such a sign from me. Yet even they do not love me as I love them. If they did, then they would have become one with my oneness, which in reality is the oneness of us all.

It is love alone which can lift the veil between a lover and the beloved. Believe me, you and I remain divided by nothing but the veil of you, yourself.

What does 'you yourself' mean? When you feel hungry, you say, 'I am hungry.' If unwell, you say, 'I am not well.' When you say, 'Baba, I slept well,' 'I am happy,' 'My son died,' 'They abused me,' 'I feel miserable,' 'Those things are mine,' it is this 'I,' 'me' and 'mine' which is the veil.

It is only because of the veil of the false ego lying between us that you find yourselves involved in so many difficulties, troubles and worries, all of which disappear automatically when touched by the reality of love. When the curtain of your limited 'I' is lifted—and it can only disappear through love, and love alone—you realize unity and find me as your real self, i. e., God. I say so because it is only I, everywhere. There is really nothing like you.

It requires cycles and cycles for one to be enlightened with real knowledge of self, or God. Therefore, millions upon millions of so-called births and deaths on your part are not sufficient in themselves to lift the veil of your limited 'I.' It can be removed through love, though, in infinitely less than a split second.

All those who are true ascetics, yogis, *walis, pirs* and saints are not necessarily God-realized. Only real lovers of God, irrespective of sex, are the true *mardan-e-Khuda* (men of God). Even from among a hundred thousand such men of God, though, perhaps only one will become God-realized after many cycles . . .

No amount of rites, rituals, ceremonies, worship, meditation, penance, and remembrance can produce love in themselves. None of these are necessarily a sign of love. On the contrary, those who sigh loudly and weep and wail have yet to experience love. Love sets on fire the one who finds it. At the same time it seals his lips so that no smoke comes out.

Love is meant to be experienced and not disclosed. What is displayed is not love. Love is a secret which is meant to remain a secret save for the one who receives it and keeps it . . .

Love God and become God. I have come to receive your love and to give you mine, as I have already said. If you love me you will find me. Unless you love me, you can never find me. Do not think that you can never love me or that you can find no time to love me. I often say that I want your love. I mean it, because that is *all* that I want from you. Therefore I always tell you to love me more and more.

I have also said that you cannot love me as I ought to be loved. To do that you must first receive the gift of my love, and that gift depends upon absolute pleasure on my part in giving you just a glimpse of the reality of my self. No one can possess love by any means other than as a gift. But I give love to self and accept it myself. The giving of love knows no law save love, which by itself is the law which governs all other laws of nature.

It is always infinitely easy for me to give—but it is not always equally easy for you to receive—the gift of my love . . .

Whatever I say, I say it in all sincerity. Unquestioning obedience to me, without consciously knowing me, will bring you nearest to me. But it is impossible to obey me literally and spontaneously. If I were in your place, I myself would not be able to do that.

The best thing for you would be to obey me cheerfully. In any case, though, to obey me now when you have not yet consciously experienced my greatness is in itself a great thing. Much of the value of obedience is lost once conviction is transformed into actual, conscious knowledge of my reality. That is the purpose for which you have been called.

Obedience is greater than all the spiritual experiences, but obedience for show is worse than no obedience.

Reprinted by permission from *Listen, Humanity*
© 1957 by Sufism Reoriented

THE ONE AND ONLY REALITY

Rest assured, I definitely know from my living experience that God is the one and only reality, and that all else is illusion. All that you see and hear at this moment—this hall, our being in each other's presence, these explanations which I give and you hear, and even my incarnation as the Avatar—all this is a dream. Every night you go to sleep and have different kinds of dreams, yet every morning you wake up to experience anew the same old dream that you have been dreaming since your birth into your present life in illusion.

You will say, "Baba, we are wide awake; we actually see you sitting before us; we can and do follow what you are explaining to us." But you will admit that you would say the same thing to me if, in a dream, you found that you were near me and heard me telling you that all you felt, saw and heard was a dream.

As long as you do not wake up from a dream, you are dream-bound to feel it to be stark reality. A dream becomes a dream only when you wake up; only then do you tell others that the life you lived in the dream was just a dream. Good or bad, happy or unhappy, in reality the dream is then recognized as having been absolutely nothing.

Therefore I repeat that, although you are now sitting before me and hearing me, you are not really awake. You are actually sleeping and dreaming. I say this because I am simultaneously awake in the real sense and yet dreaming—with one and all—the dreams which all dream.

All your pleasures and difficulties, your feelings of happiness and misery, your presence here and your listening to these explanations, all are nothing but a vacant dream on your part and mine. There is this one difference: I also consciously know the dream to be a dream, while you feel that you are awake.

When you really wake up you will know at once that what you felt to be wakefulness was just dreaming. Then you will realize that you and I are and always have been one in reality. All else will then disappear, just as your ordinary dreams disappear on waking. Then they not only cease to exist, but they are found never to have really existed.

From birth to death you keep on growing. First you are young; then you grow old and die without knowing or caring from whence you came or whither you go. From "Who am I?" to "I am God" is just one long, long dream covering ages and ages in time. But this too is found never to have existed in the eternity and infinitude of your own existence, at the moment you realize your real self, or God.

Every individual here and elsewhere is the same one, ever-indivisible God. I say this because I am responsible for the whole creation. If I am not here, then not only will you not be here but the whole of creation with all its gross, subtle and mental spheres will not be here. In short, everything exists because I exist.

In your case also the whole of creation exists because you exist. When you sleep soundly, then for you everything—body, mind, world and the universe—vanishes and is absorbed in your sound-sleep state, the most-original, beyond-beyond state of God. Then your consciousness, tired of focusing on the illusion of duality, is at rest within you.

After being refreshed in the most-original, beyond-beyond state of God, your consciousness plunges you first into the dreams-in-sleep, and then you wake up once again within the dream of creation. This dream of creation emanates again and again from you and for you.

This process of repetitive sleeping-dreaming-awakening is a result of your inability to wake up in your sound-sleep state (i.e., conscious union with God). Therefore, alternately you remain asleep or keep dreaming either the dreams-in-sleep or the dreams of creation.

It is only when you wake up in the true sense (God-realization) that you find that you alone (God) exist and that all else is nothing. Only after cycles and cycles of time can one attain one's own conscious state of God and find that one's infinite consciousness is eternally free of all illusion of duality.

The whole of creation is a play of thoughts: the outcome of the mind. It is your own mind which binds you, and it is also the mind which is the means of your freedom. You are eternally free. You are not bound at all.

But you cannot realize your freedom by merely hearing this from me, because your mind contrives to entangle you in the illusion of duality. Therefore you only understand what I am telling you, and mere understanding cannot make you experience the truth which I tell you.

For that truth, you must let your mind be halted and finally rooted out. Then, as soon as you see me as I really am, everything else will disappear and you will find yourself to be your own eternal and infinite self.

Reprinted by permission from *Listen, Humanity*
© 1957 by Sufism Reoriented

REAL BIRTH AND REAL DEATH

There is one real birth and one real death. You are born once and you really die only once.

What is the real birth?

It is the birth of a 'drop' in the Ocean of Reality. What is meant by the birth of a 'drop' in the Ocean of Reality? It is the advent of individuality, born of individuality through a glimmer of the first most-finite consciousness, which transfixed cognizance of limitation into the Unlimited.

What is meant by the real death?

It is consciousness getting free of all limitations. Freedom from all limitations is real death; it is really the death of all limitations; it is liberation. In between the real birth and the real death, there is no such reality as the so-called births and deaths.

What happens in the intermediate stage known as births and deaths is that the limitations of consciousness gradually wear off until consciousness is free of limitations. Ultimately, consciousness, totally free of limitations, experiences the unlimited reality eternally. Real dying is equal to real living. Therefore I stress: Die for God and you will live as God.

Reprinted by permission from *The God-Man*
© 1964 by C. B. Purdom

THE MEANING OF LOVE

Love has no limit, but the mind is in the way. This obstacle cannot be removed without my grace. It is impossible, because mind has to annihilate itself. For example, if one were asked to jump over oneself, the most one could do would be to take a somersault! Yet it is impossible to jump over oneself; one may jump over others, but not over oneself! Thus one may want to realize 'Baba' as he really is, but the obstacle remains.

Books and discourses will not bring about one's spiritual regeneration. Mind cannot be annihilated by mind, for one cannot jump over oneself. Only by loving me as I ought to be loved can the mind be destroyed. Anyone may have love for me, but not the love I want.

My lovers may be likened to one who is fond of lions and admires them so much that he keeps a lion in his own home. But being afraid of the lion, he puts him in a cage. The lion is always encaged; even while he feeds the lion, he feeds the pet animal from a distance and from outside the cage. Baba is treated like the lion by the lovers. There is love; there is admiration; there is an intense desire to see Baba comfortable and happy; and Baba is also frequently fed by love of the lovers. But all this is done, keeping Baba segregated from one's own self. What is wanted of the lovers is that they should open the 'cage' and, through intense love, throw themselves inside the cage to become food for the lion of love. The lover should permit himself to be totally consumed through his own love for the Beloved.

In spite of all explanations and reading of books, words remain mere words. They do not take one any further than intellectual satisfaction. Only love for God works the miracle, because love is beyond mind and reason. Where then is the necessity to read? I authoritatively say: I am the Ancient One. I have been saying this to all the world. If you love me with all your heart, you shall be made free eternally.

The affairs of the universe continue to go on without being burdensome to me in the least. But the discourses and explanations on the subject of the affairs of the universe are a headache to me. The affairs of the universe continue without my paying special attention to them. They continue to work as naturally as one's breathing, to which one does not have to pay special attention. But when there is exertion, or when one is pressed to give a discourse on breathing, one becomes conscious of the act of breathing.

In the same way, when it comes to giving explanations, I feel like one who climbs a hill and becomes breathless. Giving you discourses and explanations is burdensome to me; and as discussions, discourses and explanations are also included in the affairs of the universe, the whole affair becomes more of a burden to me than ever. Playing marbles, *gilli-danda,* cricket and flying kites are also included in the affairs of the universe; but these unburden the burden. It is like coming down a hill: It is more of a relaxation than exertion. Jokes and humour are also the things which give me relaxation.

But whether I am burdened or relaxed makes no difference; for as I really am, I am beyond all this.

I will tell you tomorrow something about my work and the workers. The selected workers should be those who do real work. I want to lay stress on workers and work. Work should be done as work; otherwise it would be no work at all. I cannot tolerate egoism and hypocrisy. He who works for me does not oblige me, for he works for his own self.

The ultimate experience can be had only after the heart is completely purified. God forgives everything except hypocrisy.

I am the Light of the Universe. One day, as soon as you get a glimpse of my reality, you will come to know me; and you will get the glimpse. Very rarely one can see me as I really am; you see everything except me. You see the curtain that surrounds my reality. Fortunate are they who see even the curtain.

THE LOVER AND THE BELOVED

Beloved God is in all.

What is then the duty of the lover?

It is to make the Beloved happy without sparing himself. Without giving a second thought to his own happiness, the lover should seek the pleasure of the Beloved. The only thought a lover of God should have is to make the Beloved happy.

Thus, if you stop thinking of your own happiness and give happiness to others, you will then indeed play the part of the lover of God, because Beloved God is in all.

But, while giving happiness to others, if you have an iota of thought of self, it is then not love but affection. This tends to seek happiness for the self while making others happy.

As for example: (1) A husband's affection for his wife. The husband wants to give happiness to his wife; but while doing so he thinks of his own happiness, too. (2) A mother's affection for her child. From this affection the mother derives happiness purely out of giving and seeking happiness for her child.

Reprinted by permission from *The God-Man*
© 1964 by C. B. Purdom

SURRENDERANCE

He who genuinely surrenders to a Perfect Master surrenders completely without asking for permission to do so. He does not even expect acceptance of his surrender from the Master. Complete surrender in itself embodies the acceptance of one who has surrendered completely as he ought to have done.

Reprinted by permission from *The God-Man*
© 1964 by C. B. Purdom

LOVERS OF GOD

Before I met my Beloved in union, I lost everything—ego, mind, and lower consciousness; but thank God, as I have just said, I did not lose my sense of humour. That is why I appear amongst you like this, on your level. Yogis and saints in India you will usually find in meditation, with long beards. You would not be allowed in their presence with your shoes on, or smoking, but with me you can do all these things, because I am one with you and one of you. From tomorrow I shall work so that this visit of yours will not be merely a picnic or sightseeing.

There are three types of lovers of God. The first is the mast, who loves and knows only God. He loses all consciousness of self, of body and the world. Whether it rains or shines, whether it is winter or summer, it is all the same to him. Only God exists for him. He is dead to himself.

The second type of lover is one who lives in the world, attends to all worldly duties fully, yet all the time in his heart he knows that this is temporary, that only God exists, and he loves God internally, without anyone knowing it.

Third type, which is the highest, is very rare. Here the lover surrenders completely to Christ, to the Avatar, to the God-Man. He lives, not for himself, but for the Master. This is the highest type of lover. Unless you have such love, merely to criticize and to judge others will take you nowhere.

Reprinted by permission from *The God-Man*
© 1964 by C. B. Purdom

LOVE AND DEVOTION

Love burns the lover.
Devotion burns the Beloved.
Love seeks happiness for the Beloved.
Devotion seeks for blessings from the Beloved.
Love seeks to shoulder the burden of the Beloved.
Devotion throws the burden on the Beloved.
Love gives; Devotion asks.
Love is silent and sublime, devoid of outward expression.
Devotion expresses itself outwardly.
Love does not require the presence of the Beloved in order to love.
Devotion demands the presence of the Beloved to express affection for the Beloved.

SAHAVAS

I am the only Beloved and you are all my lovers; or I am the only Lover and you are all my beloveds. I want you all to remain happy in my *sahavas.* I am the Ocean of Love. Draw as much of this love as possible. Make the most of this opportunity. It rests with you to draw as much love as you can out of the Ocean. It does not rest with me to explain to you how you should love me. Does a husband or a wife explain to one another how to love? One thing is certain: I want to give you my love. It depends on each of you to receive it. The easy way to receive it is to forget your home, family and all worldly affairs, when you are here, and be receptive to my love. This is the first thing. The second thing is to have a good night's rest, sleep well each night and feel fresh when you come here for my *sahavas* each day. I am God; if you remain drowsy in my presence, you will miss me and your drowsiness will oblige you to remain absent from my presence, in spite of your daily attendance.

'Sahavas' means intimate companionship. To establish this companionship you should be free with me. *Sahavas* is the intimacy of give and take of love between the lovers and the Beloved. There is no need to explain this give and take, for to create an atmosphere of explanations and discourses is to mar the dignity of love which is established only in the closest intimacy.

How do I participate in the *sahavas*? I bow down to myself, I embrace myself. It is I who smile, who weep; it is Baba who sits here on the dais seat and it is Baba who squats on the ground in the tent. Baba meets 'Baba;' Baba consoles 'Baba,' pets 'Baba,' chides 'Baba.' It is all Baba, Baba, Baba. Such is my experience of participation in the *sahavas.*

Drink deep at the fountain of love, but do not lose consciousness. If you can but taste even a drop of this love—what a wonderful experience it will be! Have you any idea what this *sahavas* is? He who approaches me with a heart full of love has my *sahavas.* After I drop this body and my passing away from your midst, many things will be said about this *sahavas.* Take fullest advantage of this opportunity in the living presence of the Avatar. Forget everything else but my *sahavas* and concentrate all your attention on me. I am the Ancient One.

Reprinted by permission from *The God-Man*
© 1964 by C. B. Purdom

MY WISH

The lover has to keep the wish of the Beloved. My wish for my lovers is as follows:

1. Do not shirk your responsibilities.

2. Attend faithfully to your worldly duties, but keep always in the back of your mind that all this is Baba's.

3. When you feel happy, think: "Baba wants me to be happy."
   When you suffer, think: "Baba wants me to suffer."

4. Be resigned to every situation and think honestly and sincerely: "Baba has placed me in this situation."

5. With the understanding that Baba is in everyone, try to help and serve others.

6. I say with my Divine Authority to each and all that whosoever takes my name at the time of breathing his last comes to me; so do not forget to remember me in your last moments. Unless you start remembering me from now on, it will be difficult to remember me when your end approaches. You should start practicing from now on. Even if you take my name only once every day, you will not forget to remember me in your dying moments.

GLOSSARY

GLOSSARY

Ashram: An unostentatious establishment where the Guru and his mandali, as well as other close disciples, live. (Page 22)

Avatar: God-man; the total manifestation of God in human form. The Avatar awakens contemporary humanity to a realization of its true spiritual nature, gives liberation to those who are ready, and quickens the life of the spirit in his time. (Page 68)

Avesta: The commentary still used today as sacred scripture among the Parsis, the basic text of which was composed by the followers of Zoroaster. (Page 6)

Brahmin: A Hindu of the priestly class who is ordained to perform religious ceremonies. (Page 16)

Daaman: Hem of the robe. (Page 86)

Darshan: Being in the presence of the Guru and the sharing of his consciousness. (Dedication, page VI)

Fakir: A Sufi monk traveling from place to place, subsisting on alms. (Page 2)

Guru: Teacher. (Page 13)

Jalali: A type of mast (God-intoxicated soul) who is hot-tempered, abusive, and talks at random. (See *The Wayfarers*, page 28, for complete description.) (Page 56)

Karma: Action, movement, deed; the unmitigated law of retribution working with equal precision in "good" and "evil" deeds and thoughts, thus determining the nature and circumstances of each incarnation. (Page 68)

Makan: Literally, a house which is constructed with mortar and lime. (Page 17)

Mandali: Close ones who, without aiming for any material or spiritual benefit, serve the Guru and obey his every whim. (Page 19)

Mayavic: Of or pertaining to Maya, the divine illusion; the power of obscuring or the state producing error and illusion; the "veil" covering reality, the experience of manifoldness, while only the One is real. (Page 36)

Mukti: Liberation; identification of oneself with the ultimate reality, eternal, changeless, blissful. (Page 13)

Prem: Literally, love. (Page 24)

Sadguru: Some God-realized souls not only possess God-consciousness, but are also conscious of creation and their own bodies. They take active interest in the souls who are in bondage, and they use their own bodies consciously to work in creation, in order to help other souls in their Godward march. Such a God-realized soul is called a salik, sadguru, or Man-God. (Page 14)

Sadhu: Hindu holy man, sage, or ascetic. (Page 40)

Sahavas: Intimate companionship; the intimacy of give-and-take between lover and Beloved. (Page 80)

Sanskara: Mental impression. (Page 13)

Tir Roj: The 13th day of the month according to the Zoroastrian calendar. (Page 2)

Toddy: An intoxicating beverage drawn from palm trees. (Page 4)

Tower of Silence: A circular tower, scientifically maintained, where the Parsis lay their dead to be devoured by vultures. (Page 2)

Yazdan: Another name for Ahura Mazda, the good principle in Zoroastrianism, and opposed to Ahriman. (Page 5)

Yoga: Restraining of the mind; disciplining the activity of consciousness. (Page 13)

Yogi: A man practicing yoga. (Page 18)

Zoroastrian: A follower of Zoroastrianism, a life-affirming Indo-Iranian religion, established by Zoroaster; still living on in the Gabar communities of Persia and the Parsis of Bombay. (Page 2)

PUBLISHER'S NOTE

We would like to thank the many people who worked
so hard and gladly gave the extra effort in love that
made this book possible.